MEMOIR OF A SOLDIER OF MARY AND THE ARCHANGELS

ALSO BY FRANK A. RUFFOLO

Science Fiction Series
Gabriel's Chalice
Tres Archangelis
Xanthe Terra

Crime
Stuck in Traffick

Action Series
Trihedral of Chaos
Distruzione della Roccia

Mystery Series
Jack Stenhouse Mysteries
Blue Falcon
10048
Lady of the Harbor
Operation Retribution

MEMOIR OF A SOLDIER OF MARY AND THE ARCHANGELS

FRANK A. RUFFOLO

MEMOIR OF A SOLDIER OF MARY AND THE ARCHANGELS, by Frank A. Ruffolo

www.frankaruffolo.com

Copyright © 2023 Frank A. Ruffolo

Printed in the United States of America

First Edition, July 2023

ISBN: 979-8-9860720-2-9 (printed version only)Scriptural passages from the following:

(WEBC). World English Bible (Catholic), Public Domain, 2020 stable text edition.

(NIV). The Holy Bible, New International Version®. Copyright © 1973, 1978, 1984, 2011 by Biblica, Inc.™ Used by permission of Zondervan. All rights reserved worldwide. www.zondervan.com The "NIV" and "New International Version" are trademarks registered in the United States Patent and Trademark Office by Biblica, Inc.™

MEMOIR OF A SOLDIER OF MARY AND THE ARCHANGELS

PROLOGUE

To begin my memoir, I must first establish what a soldier is.

Noun: An enlisted man or woman who serves in an army. A brave warrior; a man of military experience and skill or a man of distinguished valor.

Source: Power Thesaurus, www.powerthesaurus.org.

All Christians are soldiers, sent to bring the teachings of Jesus Christ to the world. We do not serve in an army or military organization but are workers promoting a cause.

What follows is the extraordinary account of my journey as a writer and a devoted soldier of Mary, accompanied by mighty archangels. This memoir contains a recollection of some of the good works I have had the privilege to perform and witness, as I strive to spread the Divine messages and wisdom bestowed upon us by our Heavenly Mother and Father, with the unwavering assistance of celestial beings.

In my role as a dedicated soldier of Mary and the archangels, my mission is to illuminate the hearts of people worldwide. With the utmost devotion, I am committed to honoring the Mother of Christ, who served as the sacred vessel that cradled the Body and Blood of our beloved Savior. This duty consumes every fiber of my being.

To illustrate the power of the angels, I include a quote attributed to Saint Thomas Aquinas: "An angel can illumine the thought and mind of man by strengthening the power of vision and by bringing within his reach some truth which the angel himself contemplates."

CHAPTER ONE

My name is Frank Angelo Ruffolo. From 1995 to 2016, I had the privilege of volunteering alongside my wife, Christine, at a Virgin Mary apparition site in Hollywood, Florida. During this time, I first began to identify myself as a soldier of Mary, a title that continues to hold deep meaning for me. In the course of my memoir, I will share my profound connection with God, the Mother of Christ, and the archangels.

My journey began on January 19, 1948, in Mother Cabrini Hospital, formerly located on a hill overlooking the historic Polo Grounds in upper Manhattan, New York. Despite due date March 15, my life truly began seven months earlier. It was a miraculous start as I came into this world prematurely, astonishingly so small that my father could cradle me in the palm of his hand. I consider my survival as a preemie the first divine intervention in my life.

When I was born, medical advancements like the incubators that are commonplace nowadays were not readily available at Mother Cabrini. Therefore, as a premature infant, the doctors at the hospital expressed their helplessness to my parents, and my survival seemed uncertain. However, my resourceful mother proved them wrong. Driven by love and determination, she placed pots of steaming water around my sleeping area to keep me warm that cold winter, effectively creating a makeshift incubator at home.

Feeding me posed another challenge. My mother could not breastfeed, and the standard baby bottle nipple was too large for my tiny mouth. Hence, my mother nourished me using an eye dropper to ensure I received the sustenance I needed. Since I couldn't consume enough food through the tiny eye dropper in a single sitting, I required feeding every two hours. Consequently, as I grew stronger and healthier, waking every two hours became a nightly routine.

My mother's immense dedication and sacrifices during those early years were extraordinary, a testament to her unwavering devotion. However, she often mentioned that the seven-year gap between my brother and me was a deliberate choice, as she wasn't eager to relive the demanding schedule she had endured with me. I consider my mother nothing short of a saint for her incredible commitment and selflessness.

This early chapter of my life laid the foundation for my gratitude for the miracles that have shaped my journey.

I was raised in a typical middle-income household, undergoing several moves within New York City. We started in Manhattan, specifically Washington Heights, then relocated to the Bronx, followed by Queens, and finally settled in West Hempstead on Long Island.

My father, a hardworking butcher, owned his own business in Manhattan, and dedicated six days a week to its operation. While he worked, my mother fulfilled the traditional role of a stay-at-home mom, diligently managing our household, as was common during that time.

I was brought up in the Roman Catholic faith. My parents followed the traditional rituals of Baptism, first Communion, and Confirmation, but attending church on a regular basis was not part of our routine. During the period between my Communion and Confirmation, I distinctly recall walking to church on Sunday mornings, perceiving it more as a punishment than an act of reverence and devotion. However, it was during this time that I experienced what can only be described as a second divine intervention.

As a nine- or ten-year-old child, I had a vivid dream about Jesus Christ. In this dream, I found myself in a state of passing away, and as my spirit departed from my physical body, I was met by the loving presence of Jesus Christ. His gentle smile conveyed a profound message: "It is not your time yet, for you have important tasks and missions ahead." I woke from the dream with a sense of awe and thought, *Wow, that was incredible*, before falling back asleep.

While I could recount other aspects of my upbringing here, none are worthy of being detailed. I struggled with being overweight. I had no girlfriends, didn't attend prom, and was generally quiet and shy, blending into the background without much distinction.

When the Vietnam War broke out, I attempted to join the military but was rejected due to my poor eyesight, likely a consequence of being born two months premature. My nearsightedness was severe, to the point that I was classified as legally blind without my eyeglasses. Adding to that, I am also color blind. Cataract surgery later corrected my nearsightedness, but I still cannot see certain colors.

In 1968, I graduated from college with an associate degree in mechanical engineering and secured a job in product planning and inventory control at an electronics company. I continued living at home without giving much thought to religion, Jesus, or the Virgin Mary. Neither were angels a topic of interest in my life at the time.

CHAPTER TWO

As the sixties transitioned into the seventies, I considered myself a non-practicing Catholic. I had distanced myself from prayers, church, and any involvement with Jesus or Mary. In my twenties, I focused more on the present, feeling invincible and not contemplating God or the future. I simply embraced each day as it came.

At work, I met a young woman, and we started dating. Eventually, I proposed marriage. However, deep down, I felt something was missing. I believed I was in love, but the relationship didn't work out, and we went our separate ways. Disappointed, I continued with my life, taking it one day at a time.

In 1973, while spending time at a club I frequented, I had a chance encounter with a woman with whom I felt a strong connection. We engaged in conversation, danced, and bonded on a profound level. We dated for a while, then stopped for a short time. Eventually we reconnected, and I proposed in 1974.

This time, things worked out, and we were married in 1975. Our wedding day marked a significant event for me, as it was the first time I had stepped foot in a church in many years — too many to recall. Through the test of time, our love has remained steadfast, persevering to this very day. As we approach the grand celebration of our fiftieth anniversary in 2025, I eagerly embrace the occasion as a monumental milestone in our relationship.

After our honeymoon, Christine and I moved out of our parents' homes and settled into an apartment in Lindenhurst, New York. Then one year later, we decided to purchase a house in Massapequa.

At that same time, the idea of starting a family took root, prompting us both to consider reintroducing Jesus into our lives, since Christine had also strayed from the Church during her college years. This newfound desire led us to commit to raising our children within the embrace of Catholic teachings, and we vowed to provide them with instruction in the faith. Interestingly, the church near our house was named Maria Regina, a coincidence that also led me to ponder the role of the Virgin Mary for the first time in my life.

In March 1978, our first child, Michael, came into the world. I've often wondered about his birth date, since my original due date was the same month almost thirty years prior, in March 1948.

We baptized our son and established a regular church attendance routine to follow through on our newfound commitment to our religion. Meanwhile, my wife's family moved to southern Florida, and my father was preparing for retirement and relocation with my mother to the same area. As a happy coincidence, the company I worked for encountered financial difficulties at that same time, prompting me to explore other job opportunities.

Given our families' plans to settle in Florida and my intention to seek alternative employment, we decided it made sense for us to move as well. Conveniently, my parents had secured an apartment in Hollywood, Florida, as a temporary residence before their official relocation, which proved to be an ideal arrangement for us as well. With that in mind, I resigned from my job, Christine transferred to her company's local branch office, and we listed our house for sale in January 1979. Interestingly, at the time, we did not know that the apartment in Hollywood would be located less than a mile from the future site of a Marian apparition.

Eager to relocate, I boarded a flight to Florida and settled into my parents' apartment while my wife stayed in Massapequa with our son to pack up our house and secure movers. Amazingly, we finalized a contract to sell our house on the day of our final move, and one week later, I secured a new job as a purchasing manager at an electronic manufacturing company in Miami.

Reflecting on the swift turn of events, it seems almost unbelievable that within four weeks, I had resigned from my job, sold our house, relocated to Florida, and secured a new employment opportunity. Some might consider this a series of fortunate events or label it sheer luck. However, I am sure it was divine intervention.

CHAPTER THREE

In the years that followed, our son continued to grow, and I participated with him in the YMCA Indian Guide program. This unique initiative aimed to unite fathers and sons, emphasizing the father's role as a teacher, guide, and friend within the family dynamic.

When Michael was four years old, our family expanded with the welcome arrival of our daughter, Alicia, a creative child who quickly enriched our family dynamic

As our children grew, our involvement in the church remained steadfast, and when Michael entered his first year of religious instruction, known then as the Confraternity of Christian Doctrine, Christine started volunteering as a CCD teacher, conveniently in the same classrooms as our children.

To further engage with the church community, I became a Eucharistic Minister, and we both took on the responsibility of chairing our parish's Pre-Cana Wedding Ministry. In this vital role, we and other married couples in the parish assisted and prepared engaged couples for marriage according to the guidelines established by the Catholic Church.

Most couples we encountered through the Pre-Cana Ministry were genuinely aligned in their commitment to one another. However, we encountered a few cases where we felt the couple was not adequately prepared for marriage. Some were not willing to fully commit to the idea of merging their lives as one. One pair, in particular, wanted to maintain separate finances, with each person responsible for personal expenses with individual bank accounts. We felt this would essentially be two independent individuals sharing a roof. Therefore, we considered it our obligation to inform the priest assigned to their wedding, urging further counseling on their behalf.

Subsequently, we discovered that this couple did not proceed with their marriage. Once again, I felt like divine intervention had occurred. Both of us were grateful for our involvement in that couple's journey and for our role in averting a potential union that may not have been founded on the necessary commitment and unity.

Continuing on my spiritual path, I joined the Knights of Columbus in 1986, the world's largest Catholic fraternal organization for men, and my membership is ongoing. As part of the Knights' pledge, we show our devotion to the Virgin Mary by carrying Her rosary. The prayers of the Rosary, a devotion derived from the Latin word "rosarium," meaning "crown of roses" or "garland of roses," holds a cherished place in the Catholic faith. This revered practice involves the use of beads to facilitate prayer.

The Rosary prayers encompass the recitation of the Lord's Prayer, followed by ten repetitions of the Hail Mary, culminating with the recitation of the "Glory Be to the Father" prayer. Additionally, the Fatima Prayer may be included. Each cycle of these prayers is referred to as a decade. While reciting each decade, believers are encouraged to meditate on one of the Mysteries of the

Rosary, which represent significant events in the life of Jesus Christ.

The original 15 mysteries of the Rosary were officially established in the 16th century by Pope Saint Pius V, building upon a longstanding tradition stemming from an apparition of the Virgin Mary to Saint Dominic in 1208. These mysteries are grouped into three categories: the Joyful Mysteries, the Sorrowful Mysteries, and the Glorious Mysteries. In 2002, Pope Saint John Paul II introduced five optional mysteries known as the Luminous Mysteries, expanding the total to 20.

Throughout the course of history, multiple popes have strongly advocated for the Rosary as an integral part of the veneration of Mary within the Catholic Church. The Rosary encourages believers to reflect deeply upon the life of Christ, emphasizing the profound connection between Mary and Her Son. It serves as a powerful symbol of the Catholic belief in actively participating in the life of Mary, whose unwavering focus is always on Christ. The Rosary further underscores the Mariological theme of drawing closer to Christ through the intercession and example of His Mother.

CHAPTER FOUR

Rosa Lopez, a middle-aged, first-generation Cuban American housewife unconnected to the Church, might seem unlikely to fulfill the role of a messenger of Jesus and the Virgin Mary. However, despite an unconventional background, Heaven chose her to transcend societal expectations, to become a vessel for Divine messages and to inspire believers with her unwavering faith.

To escape Fidel Castro's harsh regime in Cuba, Rosa and her family legally immigrated to the United States in 1967. The family started out in New York. Then they moved to New Jersey and South Florida, where they eventually bought a house in Hollywood.

To help support her family, Rosa worked various jobs in Cuba and the United States, among which were songwriter, nightclub singer, and hairdresser.

Rosa's life was ordinary, and neither she, her husband, nor her two children practiced their faith. In Cuba, displays of Catholicism were frowned upon. Consequently, none of the family were taught much about the Catholic Church.

For many years, Rosa battled illness and was confined to bed. At one point, a friend told Rosa about a visit she made to visionary Nancy Fowler in Conyers,

Georgia, and Rosa was intrigued. Despite being sickly, she embarked on a pilgrimage in 1993 to visit the visionary, which proved to be a significant experience in her life. During her visit, Rosa had a profound encounter, perceiving the presence of the Virgin Mary in the branches of a tree, the only one to have that experience that day.

After returning home, Rosa began to experience visions of Jesus and the Virgin Mary in her bedroom. These visions spanned many years, lasting from 1994 until her passing in 2018. Each experience was a significant spiritual encounter for Rosa that completely changed her life. Before the visions, she was an average wife and mother, solely concerned with her family and friends. After the visions began, she dedicated her life to serving God and the Virgin, with everything else taking second place.

Rosa's initial experiences are recounted in a book titled *Encounters of Love with Jesus and Mary*, published in 2004 by Our Loving Mother's Foundation (ISBN 0-938873-14-8). In the introduction to that book, Rosa describes what happened after her initial encounter in Georgia.

"After that day, I lived in total bliss. I did not understand anything until one day, around 3:00 p.m., while saying the Divine Mercy Chaplet, Jesus and Mary appeared to me in my home. I was lying down because I was sick, and Jesus said, *"I am going to heal you because I want this place to be holy, and I want you to be a prophet of these times."* Jesus and Mary changed back and forth from one to the other, which helped me to realize they are One Heart. Jesus told me that He would speak through me and that I would be given the gift of healing the sick who would come. He told me to dig a well for healing. The biggest miracle and triumph [I received that day] was my conversion."

This experience marked the first point in Rosa's journey as a visionary. Encouraged by the Heavenly directive, she, along with volunteers who came to the apparition site after hearing about her visions, faithfully began documenting subsequent messages from Jesus and Mary. This decision proved instrumental in preserving and sharing the profound wisdom, guidance, and love conveyed through these Divine communications.

By faithfully directing the recording of the messages, Rosa ensured that the words of Jesus and Mary would be preserved for future generations. This act of devotion and obedience allows others to benefit from the profound insights and spiritual teachings imparted during these extraordinary encounters, inspiring countless individuals on their own spiritual paths.

The first message in Rosa's book is from the morning of January 1, 1994.

"My daughter, I am your Loving Mother, who comes to give you the message for the year 1994.

"Beloved daughter, this year will be the year that will test the faith of mankind and the world. Great catastrophes will occur — earthquakes, floods; there will be changes in many governments.

"In Peru, the President will suffer an attempt on his life but will be saved. There will be problems with the guerillas of Sendero Luminoso [The Shining Path].

"In Nicaragua, it is possible that Violet Chamorro, will be overthrown.

"In Cuba, your beloved land, My dear child, and in America, there will be much uprising from the people against its leaders. Finally, the people of Cuba will see the light and it is

likely that a blow from the military will destroy the bad one; his head will roll and he will not be able to escape the anger of the people he has so mistreated.

"Cuba will have to return to God and His Loving Son, as well as to Beloved Mary, because Cuba, My daughter, hung Me in a closet just like My Son, who was re-crucified [there], and they embraced an anti-Christian system. They must pray, pray, pray. My little children, embrace the Cross, and Our Loving Mother's Rosary. Only through prayer will you be able to reach My Loving Son.

"I have spoken, dear daughter. I am your Loving Mother, who loves you the most. Make the Sign of the Cross when you are done writing. My Loving Son and I will bless you. Amen.

"Note: A great tragedy will shake Los Angeles, which will be the precursor of other tragedies because, My dear child, Los Angeles is like Sodom and Gomorrah, where all vices come together. Great idols are worshipped, and corruption is so great. My child, only God can forgive them by means of repenting and prayer to My Immaculate Heart and the Eucharistic Heart of My Loving Son and His Divine Mercy.

"I am calling you whenever I appear. Some come out of curiosity and others, at the least, come looking for proof. Only those with a clean heart will see their Loving Mother, and only those who have faith will be saved. Make a chain of prayers from Earth to Heaven. My Loving Son awaits with Loving Arms, those of clean souls and contrite hearts by means of His Loving Mother's Rosary. [The] only True Path is prayer, conversion, humility, fasting, sacrifice, repentance, charity toward the less fortunate, love between brothers, because all are My children. My Hands are filled with blessings for all if you repent and return to the love of Christ, to the unity of family. The family is the foundation of love for My Loving Son. You

must pray to stop abortion and the abuse of children, of the elderly. Whoever makes an act of charity toward one in need is doing it to My Loving Son.

"I bless you in the Name of the Father, the Son, and the Holy Spirit. Amen."

Rosa's spiritual journey on Earth involved meticulous preparation leading up to the momentous day when the monthly messages would be shared with the world. At first, Rosa received only private messages. Then, in 1994, the messages were given publicly until 2016, when Rosa's health began to deteriorate too much to continue.

Throughout this period, Rosa received numerous daily lessons and communications, providing her with invaluable guidance and personal support. These teachings played a crucial role in helping her navigate the challenges she faced, including struggles with faith and familial discord, as her newfound role as a visionary and prophet clashed with her family's expectations, particularly those of her husband.

One specific incident vividly captures the tension within her household, especially in the early years.

Over time, Rosa began to transform her home into a place of prayer and reflection, drawing pilgrims driven by faith or curiosity. To create an atmosphere conducive to devotion, Rosa adorned the walls of her house with multiple images of Jesus and Mary. However, her husband, displeased by the transformation of their home into what he perceived as a "church," demanded that she remove the paintings and images. Initially, Rosa refused. But she later complied, seeking to maintain peace in her family.

Not long after restoring her home to the way it was, Rosa experienced a profound intervention. Awakened during the night, she was instructed by Jesus and Mary to put the paintings back in their rightful places. She lay in bed, wondering how to approach her husband, when she noticed flashes of light emanating from the main area of the house. Curious, she ventured out to investigate and discovered beams of light flashing from the walls where the images had once hung. In spite of this supernatural occurrence, Rosa returned to bed without restoring the paintings.

Later that night, the whole house shook like an earthquake, startling the couple. To check the house, Rosa's husband tried to leave the bedroom, but the door wouldn't budge, so he exited through the window and circled the house, reentering through another area. To his utter amazement, he found that the closed bedroom door was blocked by a pile of the living room's floor tiles that were pulled up and placed there, undamaged.

Shortly after this, her husband restored the paintings to their original positions.

Another supernatural occurrence in the early years took place while Rosa's husband dug the well that Jesus asked her to provide for visitors to her home. While her husband dug, someone videotaped the procedure and also took a photo, both of which show an unmistakable beam of light striking the well.

These are only two of the extraordinary events that are profound reminders of the spiritual realm's presence in the couple's Hollywood home, and Rosa's unique connection to it. They showcase the Divine support she received from Jesus and Mary, reaffirming her role as a visionary and providing her with her unwavering faith in the face of adversity.

CHAPTER FIVE

As previously mentioned, Rosa, with help from her volunteers, documented the early messages she received in her book. These messages offer a glimpse into the profound guidance and support she received from Jesus and Mary from 1994 to 1995, a crucial period of her spiritual journey. Those messages provide readers with a deeper understanding of the profound wisdom and love imparted by the Son of Man and His Divine Mother. In book form, they continue to inspire and uplift countless individuals seeking spiritual enlightenment.

The following are a selection of messages from 1994, the year the public apparitions began.

January 18, 1994

"Beloved daughter, take your pencil and write. The world does not want to understand that God is God, and there is nothing in the universe that the Hand of God cannot destroy when My Almighty Arm strikes.

"Beloved daughter, don't think that I do not suffer when I have to punish My children for being disobedient. Yes, My daughter, disobedience.

"*California and Los Angeles are like Sodom and Gomorrah. All kinds of vices are found there — idolatry of persons, satanic cults, moral aberrations — that only God, if they return to Me, will forgive, if they ask from their hearts. However, they get farther away from My Mercy every day.*

"*It is, then, that I punish with a firm Hand. No, beloved daughter, when punishment arrives it cannot be avoided that innocent people fall. Innocents are the ones who do not get involved in those horrendous acts.*

"*That is why My Loving Mother appears in many places and will continue appearing until the world understands that only by My Mother's Hand will they be able to come to Me.*

"*Strongly embrace My Loving Mother and the Rosary. Pray, My dear children, make a chain of Rosaries from Earth to Heaven. Pray to My Divine Mercy.*

"*Through prayer, you will receive many blessings. This generation will not pass without seeing what will happen because of the disobedience of My children.*

"*In all places, I call you through My Loving Mother, but many come out of curiosity and not for love of the Virgin. Many believe that the miracles are for all, but I tell you that only those with a clean heart and generous soul for the kindness and love of Christ, will see.*

"*Follow the Divine Signs. Where Jesus and Mary are, is the Cross, the Holy Spirit, the angels, Padre Pio. Where the Celestial Court is, there is Divine Mercy.*

"*Come to Me through the Rosary of My Mother, and I Jesus, will listen. I bless you, My daughter. I am Jesus.*"

February 10, 1994

"My child, My dear child, you don't know how happy it makes Me to see you so happy at seeing the apparition [vision] of My rosary in your room. But you must know, dear child, that you will see many things, and many more things will happen so that people can convince themselves that I and My Beloved Son appear in your home.

"My dear child, I bless you, and My Beloved Son also blesses you. Do not worry about anything, everything will be as it has to be. Remember, dear child, everything that happens to you is already written. Many will come here, and many will see and be healed.

"I bless you, dear child. I have spoken. I am your Loving Mother."

February 16, 1994

"My child, My dear child, it is I, your Loving Mother, the One Who loves you most. I told you today that I wanted to speak to you every night and that I want you to write it down. Well, dearest child, I want to tell you many things, but I will tell them to you little by little so that you can write them, because I want you to write a book of My Messages. I want you to do it together with that stubborn man that is here in your house, which now is also My home and the home of My Beloved Son. Do not think, dear child, that what you are writing is a game. They will be messages where My Beloved Son and I will tell you everything that you have to do and everything that will happen in the world if they do not change their behavior.

"The purpose of these messages is to bring mankind

closer to My Loving Hand and to My Son. I want My children to come close and to listen to everything that My Beloved Son has reserved for all those who take My Hand.

"My child, I give them the opportunity to return to the love of My Son, to good principles, to the family. Mary and Jesus mean love, They mean peace, They mean understanding. No one can come close to My Son if their hearts are full of bitterness, full of hate and revenge.

"All I ask, dear children, is that you take the rosary. Each bead means purity of the soul, love, forgiveness, sacrifice, humility. Clean your hearts and come with humility, with contrite hearts and the soul as pure as a child, and you will receive all the blessings that My Beloved Son and I, your Loving Mother, have reserved for you.

"My child, I have not finished. It is not your mind dictating to you. It is I, your Loving Mother, or do you not recognize Me? Listen, dear child, if this generation does not change its way of life, they will not have enough time to repent of what is to come. 'Many are elected, but few are chosen.' Do not be afraid, My dear. He who does not listen to My Call here, or wherever I have another child receiving My Messages, when He knocks on the door, My Beloved Son will respond 'I have never seen you. I have never known you.'

"Dear child, I need many prayers, many Rosaries for all of My intentions and for My Son's, for the conversion of the unconverted world.

"I love you, My child. My Beloved Son and I bless you in the Name of the Father, the Son and the Holy Spirit. Amen."

February 17, 1994

"My dear child, My little one, I am your Loving Father, your Divine Mercy. Dear child, I know what you are suffering. I know you are desperate. The world is falling apart at your feet, but do not fear, I am here by your side. Nothing will happen that does not have to happen. Your husband will not get what he wants. This is the home of the Holy Family; it no longer belongs to him nor you. Do not fear, child. My Loving Mother and I will make him bend his knees and he will ask you for forgiveness. He must not think that he can play games with God. If he is not convinced that I am here, We are going to prove it to him.

"Sleep in peace, My child. I am your shelter, your shadow, the One Who shelters you. My Mother is My love multiplied. Who is against me? Do not fear. Nothing will happen, remember it. Hold onto My Hand and the Rosary of My Mother. Have faith, much faith. Everything will pass, only God remains. I bless you, My child."

February 18, 1994

"Listen, dear child. This night I want to speak to you about very important matters. It is I, your Loving Mother.

"I want you to know that you were chosen, not by Me, but by the Father, who was moved with the Holy Spirit when everything was created. God, dear child, is Who chooses His children, not His children, who choose God. As you can see, it seems simple, but it is not. The prophets were chosen by God before creation. It would be those prophets who, through the wisdom that God sent them with the fire of the Holy Spirit, who would have to lead the flock to the horizons of tomorrow. First, it was Noah, who through God Who spoke to him, warned of the flood. He was able to save the chosen few when God flooded

everything with water, and for forty days and forty nights they navigated until they found land that they could populate. It was not by coincidence; it was because it was written to be that way.

"The Bible, dear child, is filled with important events that were written by the prophets whom God utilized so that Divine messages of the things that would happen on the Earth to humanity would reach mankind, and so they would remain registered in history. There is the Book of Isaac and the Book of Enoch, one of God's most loved servants. There is Leviticus, and to be brief, there is [also] Moses, who led the Jews from Egypt to the Promised Land. Take notice, dear child, that all were chosen before they were born. How did the Father speak to them? By the way of signs. Some in dreams, others heard the voice of the Thunder of the Lord. That is how, dear child, the books were written that would remain in history to give faith in God, of how He created the universe, and who were His chosen ones, because there were many.

"Notice how the descendants of King David were chosen. My Son is a direct descendant of the Davidian Kingdom, and I, your Loving Mother, a simple girl from the outskirts of Jerusalem, was chosen to be the Mother of His Only Begotten Son. Would you want such a blessing? That is why, dear child, I wanted to tell you these things, because I want you to know that nothing happens by coincidence, everything is written. What you are going through, all the chosen ones go through. No one believes them; they have problems with everyone because he who does not see nor hear, believes that the one who sees and hears, is crazy.

"You have to have patience. Do not obligate anyone to believe. Your home is of prayer and of apparitions and you are Our messenger. Your mind is Ours, My Son and I, and in your

home, there will be great miracles. You will see, dear child.

"My beloved Son and I bless you. Your husband will bend his knees."

February 20, 1994

"My dear child, I know how busy you are by trying to accommodate all of the pictures you have taken of Us in your house. I want you to know that it looks very nice. [Rosa and others had taken photos depicting miraculous images, which she displayed on the walls of the apparition room.] *I am very happy, dear child. I want you to know one thing: Everything that My Beloved Son and I, along with the Holy Spirit, are giving you, are very Sacred things. It is not a game. My child, I don't want you to worry about things that are not important, for example, the problems of Rosa, Our friend.* [Rosa V. is a personal friend of Rosa Lopez, the visionary.] *She will see because that is how it will be. Tomorrow, everything will be beautiful because she will see Me and be able to take a picture of Me because it is the only way that people will find out that I and My Beloved Son are here.*

"My child, I also want to tell you that everything in your house is blessed by My Son, the Holy Spirit, and I, and the Name of My Beloved Son also blesses it. My child, the fountain at your house is blessed, even if you do not believe it; I see it in your face. The water in the fountain will heal those who drink the water from it. My child, that sigh is the Paraclete that gives faith. What I am telling you is not your imagination. My child, when will you convince yourself that it is Us Who are speaking to you? All the corners of your house are blessed. Everything will be as it is written. You will convince yourself when you see the people come to your home because the news will spread like

fire. You will see, My child. Don't think that this is a game. Never doubt Me or My Beloved Son. I must tell you though, that the Crucifix you placed on the Cross is very nice. The Cross, the wood, was chosen very well. Thank you, child. All those who touch it will receive blessings, never forget it. Remember, dear child, you have many gifts. Learn to use them."

Jesus: *"Child, My Mother and I bless you. Make the Sign of the Cross when you are done."*

February 20, 1994. The Message Continued that Evening.

"My dear child, remember that you and I have a meeting every night. My child, I am preparing your soul and your heart for all things that are coming. You have to have everything in order regarding what refers to Me and My Beloved Son. You know, My dear, that Our Heart is impatient to appear in a general vision for all of your family and some of your friends, so they may be convinced that it is true that We are here. But for the moment, only you will see, for you are a visionary. That is why We chose you. You were predestined for this from birth.

"In your home there will be great miracles, but the moment has not yet arrived because the conditions have not yet been given. We want to test your husband. We want him to understand that he cannot be more than God, that God has chosen this to be a house of prayer, the home of the Virgin Mary and Her Beloved Son Jesus. Is it that he has not seen the Holy Spirit give grace in abundance? Can he deny that he has seen Me? No, My child. He will have to obey and give thanks for so many blessings."

Rosa: "I asked the Virgin if it was true that I had to place the Cross next to Her Image, and She said, 'My child, everything you do is guided by the Holy Spirit, Who leads you* *by the hand.'"*

Rosa: "The Cross is so humble."

Mary: *"It cost you very little, but it was well chosen."*

Rosa: "Sometimes I ask myself, Mother, do I really hear Your Voice speaking to my mind?"

Mary: *"Yes, My child. It is the only way. Imagine if you heard another voice speaking inside your head. Then, you would go crazy. That is the medium that We use to speak to Our chosen children, the visionaries. My dearest one, rest, you have a lot of work to do for Us, your Heavenly Parents."*

Rosa: "I wanted to know something else about the Crucifix."

Mary: *"The Crucifix on the Cross and everything else will be blessed by the priest and by Us, the same as the water fountain in front of your house. Then, My child, will be the great moment. To Our beloved Rosa V., tell her she will be one more member of Our Sacred Family here. She will have visions and apparitions. Tell her not to worry about her sister; everything will turn out well. He who is with God has everything, nothing is lacking.*

"I have spoken, dear child. I am your Loving Mother, Who blesses you along with My Beloved Son. Everything you have done for Us today is very beautiful."

March 4, 1994

"My dear child, it is I, your Loving Mother. You do not know how I suffer when you suffer. But now, dear daughter, there are a lot of things I want you to know, because I want you to start on the projects that We are going to be doing in your

house.

"Listen very well, daughter, because this is very important. You have to move your room to the back [of the house] until it is possible to move you to a place close to here, because this house will remain as a Temple of the Holy Spirit of My Son and Mine.

"There will be great manifestations here that people will see of My miracles and of My Son and the Celestial Court that will appear here.

"No, do not feel sorrow for having to leave your room, it will only need to be at night, because you will be here during the day in the apparition room, giving My Messages and My Loving Son's. Well, My daughter, if you do not change [rooms], you will have a lot of rearranging to do, if they can be done; that can be done at your discretion. Wherever you may be, your Loving Mother and My Loving Son will be. [Rosa's visions started in her bedroom, which was at the front of the house. However, she was instructed to move her bedroom to the back, because her former bedroom would become the apparition room.]

"To begin with, I will tell you that this room has to be well ventilated for the sick who will come. The door can be of glass like you want, in the front. From inside here, you will speak to the people. The Virgin will remain the same. When I come, My Image will transform [on the statue in the apparition room] and you will be able to talk to Me. Many will see Me and will be able to take pictures. It will be like in many places where I appear, everything will be the same.

"The well is blessed. You will place many faucets so that people can get water. The fountain has to be clean, and the water has to run all the time — the water will always be

purified. People will be anointed and healed there. [A pilgrim donated a large fountain with a statue of the Virgin Mary at the top that Rosa placed in the front yard of her house. The water in the fountain came from the well that Jesus told her to dig, which was blessed by the Holy Spirit.]

"The Cross, where it is, is a Holy place. My Loving Son is there. Everyone who touches it will receive great blessings. On the patio, there will be changes, because another Cross will be placed there with the Via Crucis. Where one of the windows is, a door will be made, also of glass. I want everything to be to your liking.

"I know you want everyone to participate in miracles, I like when you are that way.

"Well, My daughter, We will continue to give you instructions. Everything will turn out how My Loving Son has disposed, and disposed it is. So be it.

"I bless you. I am your Loving Mother. A loving greeting for Rosa V., to wait. Everything shall come to pass."

March 7, 1994. First Message of the Day.

"My little child, I know that it seems strange to you, that while you are busy with the grandchildren and chores of your house — I mean, Our house, the house of My Loving Son, the Holy Spirit, and of your Loving Mother — We have an appointment at night, but, My daughter, I have something important to tell you and that is the final word.

"My little child, I want you to understand something: that you were chosen by God for a very important purpose. The purpose is that in your home there will be many conversions, healings, and many miracles. It is there where the Holy Spirit is

residing for the benefit of this community, and in all places. It is there where My Loving Son will shed all His Mercy, all His Love, and all the blessings that My Loving Son has given to Me to give to all of My children.

"My Rosaries, dear child, will be on the 13th of each month, beginning in May and starting at 3:00 in the afternoon, because it is at that hour when My Son shed all of His Blood and Water from His Body for humanity, to wash their sins and direct them by His Hand to their Almighty Father.

"If they [mankind] do not return by way of My Loving Son, they will never enter into Heaven. By way of His Mother, they will go to the Son. Always remember that the Holy Spirit moves everything, and without Him, nothing has been conceived.

"Dear daughter, that is why you cannot go to your country [Cuba], because your commitment is with God, with His Loving Son, Jesus, with His Loving Mother, and with the Holy Spirit, all received in the sacrament of confirmation. But all, My daughter, do not have the seven gifts of the Holy Spirit, Consoler to the chosen to deliver His Message to the world.

"We must pray, pray a lot. The Rosary and [other] prayers are the only vehicles that humanity has to walk hand in hand towards My Beloved Son.

"Pray, My children, pray for the unconverted, for the poor in spirit, for the souls in Purgatory, for the abused children, even the ones in the wombs of their mothers, for the elderly, for the incurably sick, so that they may receive blessings before leaving this world and meeting with My Loving Son.

"I bless you, My daughter, you and yours. To Rosa V., tell her that I love her and bless her. Amen.

"My daughter, you ask Me how you will give the message in May if you have to take your brother to Conyers, as you had promised. I answer you; I release you from that promise because I am here. What more do you want?"

Rosa: "I responded, 'Thank you, Mother and forgive my ignorance.'"

She responded, *"I love you."*

March 7, 1994. Second Message of the Day.

"My dear child, I am your Blessed Mother, your Loving Mother, however you wish to call Me. I have told you that I have many faces, like My Loving Son. In the places where I appear, I take the name that My Loving Son gives to each apparition site, because, dear daughter, I am a servant of God, and My obedience, My child, when God named Me Mother of His Only Begotten Son, was in total obedience — I became a real servant, so that through Me, His Word would come to pass. I had faith, a lot of faith. I knew that I had been chosen, and I abandoned Myself to the design of the Holy Spirit, the Consoler, My Spiritual Spouse, and do you know what all that meant to Me during that time when women had to obey their fathers who arranged their children's weddings from they were in their mother's wombs? My daughter, can you imagine what I suffered when the Holy Spirit presented Itself and said, 'Blessed are you among women, chosen by grace by the Eyes of God and you shall conceive, by means of the Holy Spirit, a Son Whom you shall name Jesus?'

"I, who had never been touched by any man, and [imagine] what Joseph felt, to whom I was engaged to marry.

"My child, you cannot imagine anything because in

those times, My child, whoever disgraced the man whom she was to marry, was given a bad reputation and stoned to death. Nevertheless, My child, I had faith, a lot of faith, and God spoke to Joseph and he understood, and he submitted himself with obedience, humility, and a lot of love. It was love that moved God to create in a poor Jewish girl, His Loving Son for the salvation of the world. Do you know, daughter, how I suffered when I had to see Him die tortured on the Cross, humiliated, insulted by the people who saw Him be born and do miracles? It is what He was predestined for and again, faith made Me strong, and I believed that He would resurrect and that I would see Him again.

"Dear child, I tell you this because I know how you feel after I told you that on the 13th of May at 3:00 in the afternoon, you would be making My messages public, and that the people could come and take pictures and receive miracles from the well and see apparitions, as the air here is holy, by the Power and Grace of the Holy Spirit.

"My dear child, everything will be as it is written and nothing can change what God has ordained it to be, and so it will be, daughter. Nothing will be able to change what is written in the Book of Life. Have faith, My child, neither My Loving Son, the Divine Mercy, nor I are going to defraud you — all will receive blessings on that day.

"Remember that on the other occasion it was a test; now it will not be that way. This place will be blessed, and you and those who have faith and trust will be blessed, together with their families.

"I love you, daughter, do not be afraid. I am here and so is My Loving Son. Tell Rosa V. that I am very happy with her. Because of her faith and love, she will be very blessed by My Loving Son. She, My child, will be very blessed. Well, My child,

make the Sign of the Cross before I leave. Amen."

March 7, 1994. Third Message of the Day.

"My dear child, what I want you to understand is that what has been written, is written. You are afraid that this is all false and that it is all in your mind and that it is not possible that My Loving Son has given you proof that you are one of the chosen ones. No one has received as much as you have in such a short time; and we test you in many ways.

"Everything you have suffered in your life, My child, everything has been predestined to happen, nothing is by coincidence, everything is written in the Book of Life. I want you to, with love, believe that God chose you and with that [thought] you should be happy. I do not want you to doubt, dear daughter. Your Loving Mother is not deceiving you and My Loving Son is a God of Mercy, of Love. Pray, pray, pray, dear child, so that the Holy Spirit gives you the gift of understanding, and [you will] know the reason why you were chosen. Amen, dear daughter. I love you."

March 8, 1994

"My dear child, yes, it is I, your Loving Mother, Who is anxious to speak to you, but you, dear child, entertain yourself with looking at things that have nothing to do with Me.

"Dear child, everything has been prepared for My apparition in your house, everything has been arranged for this moment, even if you don't believe it. It will be a vision that many will be able to see and many will be able to take pictures of.

"My child do not doubt; what will happen, will happen. All those sighs, My child, is the Holy Spirit that dwells within you. My child, learn to use the gifts that Our Almighty Father has given you. You do not know how many things you can do with those gifts. My child, you can place your hands upon a sick person in the Name of the Father, the Son, and the Holy Spirit, and the person will be healed from what ails him. You must know, My child, that the Love of My Son is so great that He has endowed you with the power to speak from My Mouth to others. You can see Me whenever it is necessary. You will also be able to know things about the world before they happen, and be able to announce it. How My Loving Son loves you, that He chose your home to be the home of the Holy Spirit, of His Loving Mother, of Padre Pio of Pietrelcina.

"My daughter, My Son's Mercy is so great that He has erased all the sins of your life, of your loved ones, so as to make you pure in His Eyes and worthy of His Divine Mercy. Dear daughter, love My Beloved Son very much, love very much what He represents in the life of each human being. Try to always shelter under My Mantle, all those who come in search of My love, healing, and conversion. The more they unite in pilgrimages to Mary and My Loving Son, there will be many Rosaries that will save the world from the catastrophes that are close by. The world must turn back, return to the Divine Love of God and His Loving Son. Conversion, conversion, prayers, prayers.

"My daughter, with you, My and My Loving Son's other apparitions will be fulfilled. There will be many until the world returns to the Love of God, of His Son, and Me; by way of My Hand, I will lead them to Him."

Rosa: "I asked our Loving Mother, Why do you speak so much to me? Your messages are always short."

Mary: *"Because I try to prepare your soul and your senses for Our apparition. I have spoken, My daughter. I am your Mother, the Immaculate Conception, your Loving Mother. Tell Rosa V. that I love her. She must learn to be patient and obedient. Amen."*

March 12, 1994

"My dear child, I want to speak to you now. I know you are very tired and have to get up early so you can receive the first pilgrims of Loving Mary and Her Loving Son.

"I want you to know, dear child, that after tomorrow, the apparitions will begin to spread, and then more and more believers will come to receive miracles.

"The water [from the well that was dug at the house], *dear daughter, is blessed, and you will heal many. Do not worry when an authority* [a city utility worker] *comes to analyze the water. He will not find anything wrong with the water, on the contrary, they will be surprised that the properties are the same* [as the city water]. *In addition, dear child, when they receive healings, they will have to register it to be sent to the pope.*

"My little daughter, you will see how everything changes. Your husband is becoming tamer, and that is nothing. He will submit even more when he sees what he needs to see. He will no longer deny My apparitions.

"As for your brother, do not be afraid, he will not leave. As for Rosa V., tell her, as always, she doesn't have patience, she needs to learn to wait, that things are not as easy as she believes. I love her, and I want her strong and compassionate.

"I am very happy and My Son, too, because your confessor is coming to bless the house and My apparitions.

I congratulate you for your grandson, who will be baptized tomorrow. It is in this manner that they get closer to My Loving Son.

"Well, My dear, I and My Loving Jesus, bless you and your family. Everything will be as it is meant to be. Tomorrow, be calm. I await you here as always, but I will [also] be with you and your grandson.

"Until tomorrow, dearest child, I am your Loving Mother."

March 13, 1994

"My dear child, I am here like every night, waiting for you to recognize My signs that I have something to tell you and that I am here. But you pretend not to notice because you believe that it is your imagination, until you convince yourself that I will not leave you alone if you do not listen to Me.

"Well, My little daughter, I do not want to scold you anymore because I know that today ou are like crystal bells ringing, full of happiness, giving Me and My Son thanks for the happiness of your beloved grandson's baptism. We, in Heaven, My Loving Son and the celestial angels, were also filled with joy because an angel [Rosa's grandson] has come closer to Me and My Loving Son and became a Christian. We are very happy, daughter; We are with you.

"You have seen how prayers reach the Heart of My Loving Son, and that is nothing. You will see many more things that will amaze you because you are like a little girl that has obtained something that she had never dreamed of.

"Well, My little child, I also want to tell you that the Holy Spirit poured blessings in abundance in your home. Our

pilgrims, the pilgrims of Mary and Jesus, received something that they did not expect, that is why you read the message. As I surprised them, I surprised you. In this way, they left more convinced, and you realized that you do not govern yourself. All your actions are inspired by the Holy Spirit, the Consoler, nothing that you do is by your own will; it will be My Loving Son and the Holy Spirit.

"As for your husband, I can say nothing until he does everything he has to do. He has offended God very much with his doubts and disobedience, but he is beginning to gain indulgences.

"As for Rosa V., I can tell you that I am very proud of her. Her work in spreading the news is very important.

"The messages are not to be guarded or hung on a rack, they are for the good of humanity. The world has to know that there is no salvation if it is not by way of prayer.

"Prayer, My daughter, is the most direct way to be in harmony with My Loving Son. Each bead [of the rosary] is like a spring of fresh water where My children quench their thirst and wash their sins. You must pray, pray, pray.

"Come closer to God through My Loving Son in His Divine Mercy. Pray, pray. Jesus and Mary are here to listen to you and give you Their blessing.

"I bless you and those who come here and believe."

March 19, 1994. First Message of the Day.

"Daughter, beloved daughter, My little one, you do not know how it saddens Me to see you sad. When you are sad, it is as if My Heart were torn apart, and My Loving Son also suffers.

We do not want you to suffer, and We do not want you to feel small in front of adversities. Everything [bad] that happens is of the malignant one, who does not want your things to turn out right and [wants] to obligate you to desist from the path outlined by My Loving Son.

"Rosa, My daughter, all of your sins have been erased from the Book of Life. We are cleansing you and purifying you little by little, just as a diamond is refined. And do you know what for? So that you may be worthy of My Loving Son, and so that — and hear Me well — so that you never depart from the path outlined by God, by My Son, and by the Holy Spirit.

"Sufferings, My daughter, purify the soul and [it] comes closer to God. It is by suffering that we remember that God exists. If you had everything, maybe you would not remember that God exists. If you had everything, maybe you would not remember Him, because that is how all beings are.

"Well, My daughter, never let anything that you do for your Loving Mother weigh heavily on you. Giving is how you receive, and receiving is how We give with more pleasure.

"I want you to know, My child, that the fountain is very good. You will see how many people will leave here healed. Everything is turning out as it was written it would. That is what you were born for, and it is what you will live for.

"I will tell you something very important — that news is already spreading, and soon you do not know how many people will come. Do not reject any help that is offered to you, My daughter, because those helps are for your Loving Mother and others. Listen to this one thing, My daughter — you must leave your pride of self and think only as a visionary of the Virgin Mary, of Jesus, Jesus, Jesus."

Rosa: "Mother, I am a disaster, I do not know what to

think."

Mary: *"My daughter, the malignant one puts that into your head. You must fight against him by thinking of Me, Who am at your side, and of My Loving Son, Who will guide you by way of the Consoler, and in every moment, will show you what to do and say. This is what We are preparing you for.*

"I am very happy with the flowers that your son's mother-in-law brought. They are exquisite. She, too, will receive blessings and will be converted.

"I love you and I bless you along with My Loving Son, and [I bless] all who listen with love to My Messages. Rosa, Rosa, your joy is My joy. I know you await My messages impatiently. Thank you for your part in the well. All that you do for Me will be blessed.

"I, your Loving Mother, bless you in the Sacred Name of Jesus. Amen."

March 19, 1994. Second Message of the Day.

"My dear child, you do not know how happy I am in your home today, the home of Mary and My Loving Son, Jesus. All who come today will receive great blessings. Today, the Holy Spirit will be pouring blessings on all who are looking for God by way of My Loving Son.

"Dearest daughter, I know you feel ashamed of receiving money from those who contribute to My Work, but remember, it is not for you, but for the work of Blessed Mary and the Sacred Heart of Jesus. Rosa V. will be greatly blessed — her and her family. She will receive the healing she is looking for; she will find it here.

"This has been a friendly conversation, a little of what you will receive later. Let your husband be, he will be convinced that you cannot fight against God and Mary.

"I bless you all the same. Make the Sign of the Cross when you finish writing. I have spoken, I am the Blessed Virgin Mary.

"I am the Light, dearest daughter, as is My Loving Son and the Holy Spirit. I will not speak now, but you will see later, from there in the recliner, you will speak. I will bless all. Amen."

March 21, 1994

"My dear daughter, I am here with you, suffering with you about the ungratefulness of people. They [want to] find an explanation for everything. They do not know what God is capable of doing to convince the unbelievers.

"Look, My little one, all those who doubt My apparitions and truthfulness of the messages that I give here will also know that the Blessed Virgin is only one — here, there, and anywhere I appear. I am only one, the Loving Mother of My Loving Son, Jesus. Do not try to convince anyone; they will be convinced when they see the miracles. All will have to kneel before the feet of Mary, Mother of Jesus. [Even though the Virgin Mary looks a little different in the various places She appears, She is always the same person, the one Virgin Mary, the Mother of God.]

"Dearest daughter, I know how the world is and how mankind is. I even know to what extremes mankind's maliciousness can go. You already saw how Mrs. [name omitted], was calling you so much for you to tell things to your Loving Mother and ask Her questions about her problems. In *those moments, she believed, but not after just a few words from another person, who, when they have nothing good to say of someone like you, invents something bad, all because of jealousy and bad intentions. What horror, My daughter. But do not let it hurt you. You will see that, and much more, and you will be convinced that the world and man do not have forgiveness. But My Loving Son listens to the prayers of His children and of His Loving Mother, Who intercedes for all and tries to lead them by the hand, by the way of prayers towards Him, Who is the One Who gives everything and takes everything.*

"Dearest daughter, you already see how every one of My predictions are fulfilled, and that is not anything. The calling of My Son is urgent: conversion, love of one another, prayers, walking towards My Son with humility and repentant hearts.

"Dearest children, this message is the same for all. I am here, My little ones, in this holy place. Rosa Lopez is not at fault for having been chosen for Me to appear in her home. She is not responsible for God having chosen her to bring to you My messages. No one, dear children, knows God's designs and His Divine Providence. I am here. I await you here with My open Arms and My Heart full of love to give. I only ask you one thing, My children — to pray, pray, pray. Prayer is the one thing that leads to My Loving Son. Do not doubt; I await you here. The well here has been blessed by the Power of the Holy Spirit. There is proof — the pictures are here as proof. [Photos of a beam of light descending on the well were displayed in the apparition room.]

"I love you all. My Loving Son and I bless you. Make the Sign of the Cross when you hear this message. Amen."

March 27, 1994

"My little daughter I am here, even though I know that you do not want to talk to Me. You always find some kind of excuse so that I will not come. Why, My daughter, why?"

Rosa: "You know why, Mother, you know why I sometimes don't want it, or I resist."

Mary: *"Yes, dearest daughter, I know why. I read your thoughts and your soul like an open book.*

"You continue to believe that it is not I who speaks, but your imagination. You are mistaken, daughter. It is I Who speaks to you through your mind, even if you do not believe it. But I do not want to convince you now, because soon you will see with your eyes everything that My Loving Son is capable of doing when He takes the soul of one of His children for Himself — and you were chosen, even if you do not want to believe now.

"Why do you not believe, daughter? Does not the Light that Shines speak to you? You will see everything that your Loving Father, My Loving Son, has reserved for you. My little one, I do not want you to doubt, I do not want the faith that you have to diminish, but to increase by way of all the miracles you will see occurring in your home. People, dearest daughter, will come — many more.

"Daughter, is it not enough for you with everything that is in the pictures? [In the apparition room, photographs taken of angels in the sky, Divine light shining down on the well, and other miraculous images were displayed for viewing.] *Do you not think that if the Hand of My Loving Son had not poured blessings in your home and in this State, [that] you would be able to take these pictures? Ask the people to show*

you pictures of miracles that they have photographed at their homes. No, My daughter, if they come here looking for miracles, they will not see them. I can assure you of this.

"I am here, and here I will be, giving blessings to all who come with love and humility. My Loving Son, Jesus, has His Heart full of love and blessings, and by My intercession, He will pour them out by handfuls; you will see. Many will come from curiosity, but they will not see or receive. That is why, My daughter, I tell you that you must have patience and a lot of love in order to carry the cross which signifies following My Beloved Son. Many will abandon you and despise you because they do not understand what is of God. But others will bless you for being the vehicle of Mary, Beloved Mother, and of Her Loving Son, Jesus.

"But do not suffer, My daughter — more things will happen and more things they will see, and they will not be convinced. But all those who hold onto My Hand by way of the Rosary will be saved for the Honor and Glory of Mary and Her Loving Son, Jesus.

"I have spoken, My daughter. My Loving Son and I bless you by the Sign of the Cross. Amen."

May 3, 1994

Rosa: "My dear Mother, what do You want to tell me? I am Your servant and Your Loving Son's, Our Lord Jesus Christ."

Mary: *"My child, I am here to speak with you for a while because I know you ask yourself many questions and I want to answer them. Listen, My child, I do not come in a flying saucer or in an object that scientists would like to attribute*

My apparitions to. I am the Mother of God, and the same way that God engendered in My Virgin Womb His Beloved Son through the Holy Spirit, is how He makes Me appear in any place of the universe. What explanation do the scientists have to explain My apparitions throughout the world? The entire universe belongs to God. Yes, other lives exist on other planets, but God is the same in all places. He is the God of the entire universe. Nothing can move without the consent of the Creator of the Universe. Therefore, all those who deny an apparition or miracle, will be erased from the Book of Life. What does My Beloved Son Mean [by], I have not known you; I have never seen you?

"My child, who was the first one to perform a miracle? It was My Beloved Son, Jesus. The Jews denied Him; they persecuted Him, even though they knew He was the Son of God. They crucified Him, humiliated Him, they stripped Him, spit upon Him. If in these times Mary appeared, not in the form of light, but in flesh and bones like Jesus, they would crucify Me, like My Beloved Son, dear child.

"What little faith has the man of these times. That is why the Second Coming of My Beloved Son draws near in gigantic steps, and many will be called, but few chosen.

"The same thing that they do to Nancy [a visionary in Georgia] *by calling her a liar — even though they have confirmed the truth of My apparitions and miracles — that is what they will call you. For you, it will be worse because they will say that you are jealous of Nancy. There are those around here who call you a witch. I want you to know that they have even said that you are crazy. In your own family there is someone in charge of taunting you, of defaming you, of inventing all kinds of lies against you. But, dear child, the punishment for that person will be so great that they will not*

have time to repent. Remember child, fortunate are those who believe without seeing because they will see God.

"Well, My child, I take leave. I am the One Who loves you most, remember it always — Mary your Loving Mother. I will be here on the 13th, remember it. They will see miracles in the sun and [will take] the best pictures they have ever taken. My Beloved Son blesses all. Amen."

May 8, 1994. Mother's Day.

"My dear child, it is I, your Mother, the One Who loves you the most — Beloved Mary. Yes, My child, I am the Loving Mother because in Me, live all the mothers that are in the entire world. In Me, all are reflected, because I am the same in all places.

"Listen, My child, I want you to know that I am very proud of you because you are fulfilling everything that My Beloved Son has asked you to do. Never worry about what you will say at a determined moment because it will be the Holy Spirit, My child, Who will dictate what you have to say at each moment. Remember that My Son likes obedient children; they are ignorant, so that He can teach them. Be a gentle dove in His Hands of the Potter, so that He can mold, My child, your entire being.

"My Beloved Son, My dear child, knows that the path is long and hard, but He will always sustain you. When you feel tired, say, Consoling Spirit, help me with this load so that it becomes lighter.

"Your home, My dear child, is greatly blessed. Remember always that God will provide. Do not ask for anything, but what is given to you. Accept it, because it is the Work of the

Lord, in His Honor and His Name.

"Now I want to tell you something, dear child. Many things will change in your home because you will have a lot of work and you will need help from people like Maria and Rosa V. and the married couple. Your husband will also have a little more help because little by little, you will have to move everything to another room because this will be a room of apparitions. Don't think that everything will be as it has been until now because they have not yet seen the immensity of the Love of My Beloved Son which will make Me manifest Myself in Spirit and truth as a Celestial being. Many will see Me, and they will be surprised by so many blessings.

"My dear child, thank you for the love that you sow and the love that you gave, that is why My Beloved Son chose you, but as He says, do not become vain.

"Well, dear child, tell Rosa V. that the rosary on her clothes was My gift for Mother's Day for being so good, and it will always be, because she prays very much. The love that she gives Me and My Beloved Son is worthy of the gift. She will receive more if she continues on the path of Mary, Beloved Mother, and of Jesus Christ the Only Begotten, Only Son of God." [On May 7, 1994, during a meeting of various pilgrims at Rosa's house, Rosa was reading some of the messages when a rosary appeared in the form of bright light on the clothes of Rosa V. The vision of the rosary lasted about 15 minutes. Everyone who was present witnessed a great blessing.]

May 9, 1994

Rosa: "Forgive me, Father, help me, because I do not know if what I am doing is how You want it to be done.

Forgive me, Father, if I have failed You in something."

Jesus: *"My dear child, listen. I, your Loving Father, want to tell you that you are doing it well. Do not worry about anything because I will always help you come out ahead on this path that We will be on for the conversion of all America, because wherever My Mother appears, She will plant the seed of love toward My Eucharistic Heart and Her Immaculate Heart, too.*

"My child, everything is marching along in your home. You will see how everything resolves itself. I will tell you something very important. At these moments, a revolution is being born in America in an important place where the government will ruin a government in Central America.

"My child, the waters will flood many regions in different countries and also here in the United States of America, which will cause destruction and many problems. The world will have to move toward prayer in the churches, [they] will have to join hands in the love of My Loving Mother, and in one total conversion, [they] will have to pray, pray, pray, until each prayer forms a holy circle around the world so that you can love your brother next to you, whomever it may be. I love all the same, because all are My children, and Loving Mary, Mother of All, is Defender in the heavens and the Earth for all those that love My Holy Name.

"My dear child, the 13th will be wonderful for all those who come to your home. They will receive My blessings and My Loving Mother's blessings along with the Holy Spirit. Remember that My Mother will be here at any time, pouring out Her Grace for all. At 3:00 in the afternoon, the Divine Mercy will be prayed and there will be great miracles.

"I bless all of you and everything that you bring. I am

your Father, the One Who loves you all the most — Jesus. Amen."

May 13, 1994. First Monthly Message from Our Loving Mother for All Her Children.

"My dear child, I am your Loving Mother, the Virgin Mary, Mother of all — white, black, Indian, good and bad. They are all in My Heart.

"You do not know the joy My Immaculate heart feels, as well as the Sacred Heart of My Beloved Son, My Beloved Jesus, when I see how you come to the humble home of My servant, the littlest one. She is the latest one We have chosen, to use her mouth and mind to communicate with Our children.

"I want you all to know that only by My Hand and through the Rosary will you be able to go to My Beloved Son. My Son listens to all of the prayers because in each Rosary I will be there as your representative.

"My Beloved Son and I know that many will come the first time because of curiosity, and others to see if I truly appear. To all, I say that only those with contrite hearts and clean souls will see but that all will receive Our blessings because all are My dear children.

"During this year, the faith of Christians will be tested because many catastrophes will occur in the world, especially in America [Central and South America] and the United States, all because of the disobedience of My children. Only by love will they come in total conversion to My Son. In Cuba, the light will shine soon, but there will be much blood. That blood will wash away the sins of the Cubans. You remember the Roman Coliseum? Cuba became a coliseum when the

malignant came to govern. They crucified My Beloved Son and stopped believing in My Church. That is why, until Cuba returns its eyes to God and His Loving Mother, they will not be free from the malignant.

"Pray, pray. Prayer causes miracles. Your Loving Mother blesses all of you. Amen."

CHAPTER SIX

After Our Lady delivered Her first public message on May 13, 1994, my wife and I slowly became aware of a visionary living in our general area. However, despite our best efforts, we could not find the exact address. Every report we heard or read only said the location was in the city of Hollywood; nothing more specific than that. Frustrated, I began to believe that perhaps we were not yet ready or called to experience it.

Finally, a small article in the local paper revealed the address. The next apparition was said to be held on November 13, 1994, a Sunday, and we decided to seize the opportunity and attend, even though South Florida was expecting the arrival of Tropical Storm Gordon that day.

After church on November 13, dark clouds started rolling in. Undeterred, we headed to Hollywood anyway, determined to experience a possible visitation of the Virgin for ourselves. Christine's parents had been to Medjugorje twice, a small village in Bosnia-Herzegovina, where the Virgin Mary has been appearing to six teens since 1981. The stories of their encounters there were enthralling, inspiring us to investigate the local reports of a similar event here.

Upon turning onto 66th Avenue, we immediately came upon a large gathering of people. Finding a place to park necessitated us turning around and driving around the block. However, we couldn't get far because police had barricaded the intersection at which the house was located. Ultimately, we parked at a nearby office building, then walked a few blocks to Rosa's house in light rain.

When we arrived and wormed our way into the crowd, the closest we could get to the proceedings was the sidewalk across the street. Standing there among hundreds of others, we eagerly listened to the visionary addressing the crowd. Interestingly, it was not raining in front of Rosa's house.

Regrettably, we had arrived too late to hear the Virgin Mary's message. But Rosa was still speaking, instructing the crowd on matters of spiritual importance. She spoke in Spanish, and a translator relayed her words in English.

While Rosa talked, Christine glanced upward and excitedly pointed to an image of the Virgin Mary manifested in the clouds above the house. Though she tried to describe what she was seeing, I could not detect what she was referring to.

Then Rosa concluded her address and urged the crowd to join hands, emphasizing that the Holy Spirit would descend upon us all.

My wife and I clasped hands, and when Rosa said the Holy Spirit was there, I felt an intense surge of warmth and energy as if a powerful current had struck the top of my head and surged through my entire being, overwhelming me with a profound sense of peace.

Later, as we discussed our experiences on the way

back to the car, we found that Christine and I did not have the same encounters.

Thus, we departed with two distinct manifestations: Christine witnessed the Virgin Mary, and I was touched by the Holy Spirit. Christine "saw," and I "felt."

CHAPTER SEVEN

After our first visit to the apparition site, Christine started going to the house during her lunch hour every thirteenth of the month, the date of Our Loving Mother's appearances. Since she worked in Hollywood, it was convenient for her to attend, and in late 1995, she began taking the 13th day off from work every month to volunteer at the site. I joined her as a volunteer on January 13, 1996.

One apparition day soon after, I had the first of many deeply rewarding experiences.

That day, approximately 1,000 people were present, with the street blocked off as usual. Many pilgrims gathered outside the house, praying the Rosary and eagerly awaiting Our Loving Mother's visit.

After the message was delivered, people formed a line to receive a blessing from the visionary, Rosa Lopez. As my wife and I watched, we noticed that many who received the blessing were falling backward, an experience commonly referred to as Falling in the Spirit or Slain in the Spirit. I was skeptical, having seen similar things on TV. But my wife, who had been blessed before and had a powerful encounter, encouraged me to join the line.

Though doubtful, I decided to participate.

The line progressed up the driveway, which was unpaved and covered by gravel. Volunteers positioned themselves behind the pilgrims, ready to catch anyone who felt overwhelmed, to prevent them from falling onto the rough surface.

I did not expect anything extraordinary to happen to me, but I remained in place. When I reached the front of the line, Rosa made the Sign of the Cross and touched my forehead. Instantly, I felt a warm rush radiating from the point of contact throughout my entire body, and the next thing I knew, I was lying on the ground, having no recollection of falling.

The moment I realized where I was, I remember thinking, *This seems silly. Why am I lying here?* I attempted to get up but found myself unable to move. Even though I was lying on pebbles, it felt like I was on a feather bed, and I felt nothing but profound peace and comfort.

Despite my initial efforts to rise, I remained on the ground because of the incredible tranquility I felt. However, as time passed, the stones and pebbles beneath me began to dig into my back, causing me discomfort. At that point, I was able to get up.

After that transformative experience, Christine and I attended the volunteer meetings, and I joined her as a regular at the site, also taking off from work every thirteenth.

Three years later, on January 13, 1998, my wife and I

volunteered at the apparition site with other helpers as we did every thirteenth day of the month. We assisted visitors, answered questions, and shared our encounters.

Little did I know that this particular day would mark another momentous milestone in my spiritual journey. It was the day an extraordinary gift was bestowed upon me during a profound encounter with Rosa Lopez, the visionary.

As was usual during this period, Rosa summoned each of the volunteers into the apparition room to be blessed before the apparition began. During these times, I occasionally felt the presence of the Holy Spirit. However, when Rosa blessed me on this day, the Spirit engulfed me with a depth and intensity beyond anything I had experienced before. The encounter was so profound that I did not rouse from it until someone gently tapped me on the face.

As I sat up, I comprehended that I had been entrusted with a special blessing through the power of Our Lord Jesus Christ and the intercession of His most Beloved Mother, Mary. I received the profound ability to bestow the Holy Spirit upon individuals and offer them the healing grace of our Lord Jesus Christ.

The weight of this responsibility astonished me, but I accepted it with deep humility and reverence, understanding my unworthiness. I pledged to fulfill it to the best of my abilities.

At this point, I should mention that before this extraordinary event, I had noticed a peculiar pressure in the center of my palms whenever I recited the Our Father during Mass, and on this day, it also happened at the apparition site. But it was significantly more intense there, and even left distinct red marks.

I confided what happened to Rosa, and she immediately recognized the significance of the calling, advising me to seek a priest's blessing. Coincidentally (or not), the priest I asked to bless me had previously met Rosa and believed she had a special connection to Jesus and Mary.

After the apparition was over, I returned home and turned to the Bible to comprehend the extraordinary occurrence that had unfolded that day. Seeking guidance from Scripture, I providentially opened the Bible to **1 Corinthians 12:1-11**, where I discovered insights that offered profound illumination for my newfound journey: *"Now concerning spiritual things, brothers, I don't want you to be ignorant. You know that when you were heathen, you were led away to those mute idols, however you might be led. Therefore I make known to you that no man speaking by God's Spirit says, 'Jesus is accursed.' No one can say, 'Jesus is Lord,' but by the Holy Spirit. Now there are various kinds of gifts, but the same Spirit. There are various kinds of service, and the same Lord. There are various kinds of workings, but the same God who works all things in all. But to each one is given the manifestation of the Spirit for the profit of all. For to one is given through the Spirit the word of wisdom, and to another the word of knowledge according to the same Spirit, to another faith by the same Spirit, and to another gifts of healings by the same Spirit, and to another workings of miracles, and to another prophecy, and to another discerning of spirits, to another different kinds of languages, and to another the interpretation of languages. But the one and the same Spirit produces all of these, distributing to each one* *separately as he desires."* **(WEBC)**

The gift I had received was so very new to me. So as the Virgin Mary instructed, I began to keep a notebook by my bed to record the spiritual happenings and visions I was experiencing.

On Saturday, January 31, 1998, at a meeting of the volunteers of Our Loving Mother's Foundation, Our Loving Mother spoke to us through Rosa and gave special gifts to several who were there. She said the gifts would be slowly revealed to us; some would start having dreams and visions, while others would discover their gifts as needed.

As for me, Our Mother bestowed a second special gift.

While Our Lady was speaking, I felt another unusual pressure in my palms. Not long after that, I took up the task of restoring religious statues that were donated to the apparition room and in need of repair. With dedication and skill that I have come to believe I acquired at the meeting that day, I began to meticulously repair these statues, often mending or adding arms and faces, ultimately restoring them to their original beauty. Rosa, in her affectionate manner, often referred to me as her "little Joseph," as she believed my hands were given a unique blessing.

To this day, I occasionally continue this work, and each time, I am left astonished by the results. While working on the statues, I sometimes find myself convinced that they smile back at me, and when I complete the restorations, the previous damage is virtually unnoticeable.

As a group, the volunteers of Our Loving Mother's Foundation grew closer as time went on. Some who visited the apparition site conferred endearing titles upon our diverse team of helpers, though others were not as kind. Nonetheless, all of us wholeheartedly continue to embrace our shared dedication to Our Lord and His Holy Mother. We are all passionate devotees of our religion.

Along with spiritual teachings, Jesus and Our Lady often gave Rosa profound insights into forthcoming events, some of which we later verified by a story reported in the news.

Whenever the volunteers realized that something they heard or read aligned with a previous vision or message, we diligently documented and disseminated the connection through the complimentary bulletins we provided every month at the apparition site.

One such foreknowledge was a vision Rosa had the day after she received Our Loving Mother's August 13, 1995, message. Later, all of us would realize that this vision was profoundly prophetic.

Monthly Message from Our Loving Mother for All Her Children

August 13, 1995

"My dear children, My little ones, My beloved little ones, forgive your Loving Mother Who today has wanted to rejoice in your presence. Today, My little ones, the heavens feast because My Beloved Jesus Glorifies Himself in this small place where His

love makes possible what many do not want to believe. The love of My Beloved makes Me visit you to give you a little of that love He left for you for the rejoicing of all His brothers and all My children. Today, the Divine Spirit will warm you with His rays of light and love for the salvation of all who open their hearts when He knocks.

"My beloveds, the day is hot, but when My little one comes out, she will be in the company of one of Jesus' servants, John Paul, loved by all the Heavenly Court because of his humility and his love for his brothers. Jesus, My Beloved Jesus, bestows His breeze so that all may be refreshed. Rejoice, My little ones, because the times are forthcoming, and I want all My little ones to be prepared so that nothing will surprise you, but so you will be in the Light, where I will lead you to the encounter of the True Way, which is Jesus. Whoever trusts in Him will never fear what is to come because He is Love, My little ones. Love as He has loved you because many things will happen that will change the course of humanity.

"Pray, pray, pray. Remain in forgiveness and prayer. Prayer will unite you with Him and with His Love.

"I love you and bless you. I am your Loving Mother, the Virgin Mary. Amen. Everything you bring with you will be blessed. I love you."

The next day, August 14, 1995, Rosa received a series of visions at 2:45 a.m. The first was of an explosion in what looked like towering buildings where everything was destroyed, and many people died. The second was of an airplane exploding in the air somewhere in the Americas, where she saw many dead people.

Many years later, we made the connection that these visions, unveiled years prior, were eerie foreshadows of the tragic events that unfolded in the United States on September 11, 2001, a day that is now etched in the annals of history.

CHAPTER EIGHT

In this chapter, I will share a series of powerful experiences and visions I had between 1998 and 2004. These events have become less frequent since then, though they still happen today. I will also include testimonials from others who witnessed spiritual and physical healings during that same period.

One such significant experience happened to me on March 13, 1998, during Our Loving Mother's apparition.

As usual, the apparition room was filled with people, predominantly volunteers and those who were terminally ill, all devoutly reciting the Rosary.

As soon as Mary revealed herself to Rosa, I instinctively dropped to my knees, bowed my head, and closed my eyes, immersing myself in the sacred atmosphere. I began to utter the Hail Mary prayer repeatedly, seeking a deeper connection to our Holy Mother.

Slowly, in the darkness behind my eyelids, a vivid blue circle materialized, captivating my attention. Within this circle, the features of the Shroud of Turin emerged, continually transforming into unfamiliar faces before returning to the visage of Jesus. I became entranced by these mysterious faces, completely losing track of time and my physical surroundings. The vision abruptly concluded when the presence of the Virgin Mary was departing from our midst, reorienting me to the apparition room.

On another occasion, late one weekend afternoon, Sunday, April 19, 1998, Christine and I had been assisting Rosa with visitors to her home when I was preparing to close the apparition room for the day. As part of my routine, I turned off a cassette tape player that had been playing angelic-like music inspired by the apparition of Our Lady of Guadalupe in Mexico. Then, I entered the rear extension to switch off an electric fan in a far corner. As I approached the back wall, I suddenly halted in my tracks, captivated by the sound of voices singing the same melodious tune that had been playing on the tape player moments ago. The voices, sounding angelic, evoked a sense of ethereal beauty within the entire room. Curious, I returned to the cassette player and was astounded to confirm that I had turned it off. The enchanting voices persisted briefly before gradually fading away, leaving me in awe of the exquisite experience I had just encountered.

A series of other remarkable incidents unfolded during a pilgrimage to Italy in May of 1998 with Rosa and volunteers of Our Loving Mothers Foundation. The following three episodes took place during this spiritually enriching journey.

On May 24, 1998, a serene Sunday afternoon, our group, which included my wife, Christine, and her mother, found ourselves strolling through the grandeur of Saint Peter's Basilica. As we meandered past various side chapels, we encountered a Catholic Mass in progress, prompting us to join the congregation and receive Holy Communion.

During the reception of the Eucharist, the sacred host was placed on my tongue, and I made my way back to our wooden pew, as usual.

Suddenly, an intense surge of heat coursed through my body. The powerful sensation made me dizzy, and I felt compelled to descend to my knees upon the marble floor. Despite the absence of kneelers, the experience was surprisingly comforting, akin to resting on plush carpeting. In the hallowed halls of Saint Peter's, this notable moment gave me a great sense of peace.

On May 28, 1998, during that same trip, we were visiting the chapel in Pietrelcina where Saint Padre Pio first received the stigmata, when I was overcome by the Holy Spirit while praying.

The instant I perceived the Spirit over me, the palms of my hands began to hurt again. Trembling with these sensations, I left the chapel, and sat on an outside bench. Then I went back inside and knelt in prayer. Seeing me there, Rosa Lopez anointed me, and I fell into the Spirit, feeling intensely peaceful.

When the Spirit left me, I got up, but I was still shaky. That feeling lasted for about five minutes.

Later that day, I received Holy Communion at the Padre Pio Shrine in the Italian city of San Giovani Rotundo, and the Eucharist tasted very sweet, like honey. This was unusual, as the host normally has no flavor.

Then, before I fell asleep that night, I said my evening prayers and had two visions: I saw a tornado hit a factory or a long building somewhere in the United States, and I witnessed tanks rolling down a desert road.

Lastly, on June 1, 1998, I envisioned Saint Francis of Assisi calling me from a doorway while we were on the plane returning to Miami.

Visions and messages have continued to be a part of my life, leaving upon me a lasting impact. Among the many experiences I have encountered, the following are ones I consider most memorable.

The first is the vision or message I described earlier when I met Jesus Christ in a dream, and He told me that I had important things to do on Earth.

The second is a vision that occurred on the fateful morning of September 11, 2001, when I was abruptly awakened by the striking image of a solitary tree standing tall and proud, only to be suddenly engulfed by a dense cloud of smoke and debris.

I did not remember what I had seen until the day unfolded, and the tragic events of the 9/11 terrorist attacks in the United States played out repeatedly on television broadcasts, revealing the meaning of my earlier vision.

The following two visions, which occurred during meetings of Our Loving Mother's volunteers at the apparition site, also left a profound impact on me. While the exact dates escape my memory, the clarity of these visions remains etched in my mind.

In the first one, I found myself lifted into the air by the gentle embrace of the Virgin Mary. Hovering above an ancient church building, I surveyed a courtyard adjacent to it, with a dark and foreboding pit within. Compelled to explore further, I ventured into the depths of this darkness, only to be confronted by the harrowing sight of the gates of hell. The devastating despair and fear that enveloped me at that moment is indescribable. Overcome by terror, I screamed, yearning to escape, and abruptly returned to reality, my heart racing.

The second vision transported me to a heavenly court, where I assumed the role of a sentinel between towering columns of majestic marble. Before me, a vast multitude of souls filed past, each approaching to receive their final judgment. On the opposite side of this crowd stood archangels, resplendent in their pure white attire. The air was filled with a solemn silence as the thousands of souls moved in a slow procession. The weight of the moment was palpable, and I stood in awe of the divine proceedings.

Another of the visions I hold dear is particularly significant, occurring during a thirteenth day gathering at the apparition site. In the intimate setting of the apparition room, limited to about twenty-five individuals, including volunteers and pilgrims with various health conditions, I had the rare privilege of witnessing the Virgin Mary's manifestation.

As I saw Her, Our Lady was cloaked in a radiant bluish light, emanating beauty beyond description. I gazed at Her, overwhelmed by an outpouring of love, peace, and joy. I longed for Her presence to endure, even desiring to accompany Her as She departed.

However, She bid Her farewell, and a moment of sadness gripped me, immediately replaced by a tremendous surge of joy, as I had been blessed with the glorious sight of the Virgin Mary Herself.

The next phenomenon I recount did not involve me directly but is equally remarkable, as it was witnessed by a single individual who shared her encounter with Rosa and various pilgrims and volunteers at the apparition site, including Christine and me.

I recall that this particular incident took place on Saturday, January 10, 1998, while Christine, a couple of fellow volunteers, a few pilgrims, and I lingered within the apparition room, engaging in conversation and generally relaxing with Rosa.

At one point, a pilgrim arrived at the house and asked to speak to Rosa. During her conversation, she revealed that she had gone to the apparition site sometime the previous year to pray for her sister-in-law, who had been scheduled for a delicate operation. After that, she felt God answered her prayers, so she returned to thank Him on apparition day, December 13.

Over the course of the Virgin Mary's remarkable presence spanning more than two decades in Hollywood, we had the privilege of hosting numerous visiting Catholic priests who would perform Mass at the site. On that December 13, a short, middle-aged priest from New York of East Asian heritage arrived at the site clad in black clerical shirt and slacks and graciously presided over a Mass.

The woman said she arrived late that day. The Mass had already started, and due to the crowd packed into the apparition room with its limited space, she had to sit outside on a chair under the awning over the driveway. The apparition room was small; some inside were seated tightly together, and others had to stand shoulder to shoulder.

As the Mass progressed, it became time for Holy Communion, and the woman said she felt a strong urge to receive Our Lord. However, she thought she shouldn't because she hadn't attended Mass or been to confession in a long time. So, as people filed past her to receive the holy sacrament, she remained seated.

However, she said that after the last person received Our Lord, the other priest came right up to her. He held out the host, and, surprising herself, she took Communion, even though she had previously felt unprepared.

While the woman was telling this story, everyone in the room who was at that December Mass listened intently, confused by what she meant by the "other" priest.

To clarify her story, Rosa asked, "What other priest? There was only one there that day."

Confidently, the woman replied, "There were two priests there, and the other one gave me Communion."

Rosa asked the woman to describe this other priest. She said he was taller than the other one, had gray hair and a gray beard, wore white vestments, and wore gloves on his hands.

Stunned, Rosa brought her over to a picture of Padre Pio, a well-known Franciscan priest who lived in Italy, died in 1968, and had worn fingerless gloves to cover the open wounds and profuse bleeding of the stigmata on his hands. That stigmata were two of Christ's final five wounds that this cleric had suffered with most of his priestly life.

Instantly, the woman said he was the priest that gave her Communion. More astounding, upon further questioning, she revealed that she had known nothing of Padre Pio and had never seen a photo of him before that day.

Interestingly, Rosa had previously told us that Padre Pio frequently accompanied the Virgin Mary on apparition day and performed miraculous healings for people she prayed for.

CHAPTER NINE

During the twenty-two years Our Loving Mother appeared in Hollywood, Florida, countless healings and visions were experienced by pilgrims, volunteers, and us, including statues mysteriously shifting positions, celestial visions that bestowed a hint of the divine, encounters with saintly presences, images captured in the clouds, and miraculous healings that defied conventional explanation.

While I would love to recount all these extraordinary occurrences, I will only provide a glimpse into that wondrous tapestry of miracles.

For as long as the Virgin Mary appeared, tens of thousands of pilgrims from across the globe visited Rosa's humble abode. Some became devoted regular visitors, while others were driven by curiosity, a quest for truth, or a desire to dispel doubts. People of diverse ethnic backgrounds, faiths, and religious affiliations converged upon this space, united in their shared pursuit of what their hearts yearned for: hope, well-being, or perhaps a rekindling of faith in the inherent goodness of humanity. Some found their spiritual path redirected, undergoing profound conversions, while others still departed as agnostics, their beliefs unchanged, yet perhaps touched by the seeds of charity and forgiveness planted during their visit.

Many who were blessed with miraculous events were more than willing to share their powerful testimonies, which we documented in the monthly bulletins and on Our Loving Mother's Foundation website. Regrettably, this website ceased operation after Rosa's passing, but I am honored to recount some of these awe-inspiring testimonies here, as written by the recipients themselves.

Date: January 13, 1993
Name: Donald R. *(full name omitted)*
City: Hallandale, FL
Description of Spiritual Revelation:

I, myself, Donald R., born July 8, 1935, first visited the home of Rosa Lopez on January 13, 1993. I had not attended church all my life until that day, when a miracle happened to me: I saw the sun dance and spin side to side. Well, my life took a 90-degree turn. I was converted and attend Mass every week.

Praise the Lord and thank you, our Virgin Mary! I am also thankful to Jesus! Glory to God!

Date: September 19, 1996
Name: Jessica M. *(full name omitted)*
City: Pembroke Pines, FL
Description of Spiritual Revelation:

On September 10th, I had a burning in the pit of my stomach and pains in my abdomen. As the days passed, the pain spread over my entire waist. By Thursday, I was very pale from the strong pains that I had. I decided to go to the doctor, who performed blood and urine tests. The result of the urine test was negative, so my doctor sent me to have three sonograms at Memorial Hospital. He also referred me to a stomach specialist and a gynecologist. My appointments for all these tests were on Tuesday, September 17, but on the Sunday before that, I went to Rosa's to receive a healing.

Rosa asked me if I was suffering from either stomach pains, gas pains or gastritis. I responded, "Yes," and then she told me not to worry, that I was healed, and that I should drink tea made from the rose petals, plus the water of the Virgin. She also said that I should continue to go there once each week to continue the healing or that I could end up in a wheelchair.

[Note: Pilgrims often brought flowers, usually roses, to adorn Our Lady's statue, and when they died, volunteers dried them and gave them out to whomever wanted them. The water was from the well that Rosa dug at the house following Our Lady's instructions.]

On Tuesday, I kept all the appointments I had with the doctors and the hospital. The results of the three sonograms were all negative. The doctors did not understand how this could be, because of all the pain that I had. The stomach specialist had assured me that he was 100% certain that what I had was gallstones and when he called the hospital for the results of the exams, he couldn't believe that there was no problem, that the exams were all negative.

I give thanks to the Virgin and to the Lord.

Date: October 4, 1996
Name: Edna R. *(full name omitted)*
City: Aurora, IL
Description of Spiritual Revelation:

Dear friends, I am writing this to testify to a miracle I just received. An ultrasound on Sept. 12 revealed a large tumor in my abdomen. The next day, I drank a little of the holy water from Hollywood. The Blessed Mother has become very dear to me and I've been praying to her daily for 1½ years now. I have also applied holy water from Lourdes and holy water from a woman in St. Charles, IL, where miracles are also happening. Yesterday, Oct. 3rd, I received the results of the CAT scan I had on Oct. 1st and there was absolutely no trace of the large tumor. My doctor tried to explain an unexplainable event. I think he is baffled. I definitely attribute this special healing to Our Lord's abundant mercy and Our Lady's great love for me. Praise God!

(Signed) *Edna R.*

Date: November 3, 1996
Name: Wilhelm H. H. *(full name omitted)*
City: Davie, FL
Description of Spiritual Revelation:

Back in July of 1996, I suffered a torn patella ligament in my left knee. After going to Memorial West Hospital in Hollywood, FL and an orthopedic doctor, I was informed that I may need surgery and may have to miss six months of work.

My wife Cathy took me to Rosa's and she rubbed

holy oil on my knee. When I went to Rosa I was on crutches and a knee immobilizer and I had missed one week of work.

Later that day, I couldn't believe the fact that the pain had gone away and that the crutches were no longer a necessity. Today, November 3rd, two days after seeing Rosa, I have returned to work and my knee has not bothered me at all.

Thank you, Rosa. Thank you Mary, Mother of Jesus Our Lord.

(Signed) *William H.*

Date: November 10, 1997
Name: Humberto S. C. (*full name omitted*)
City: Miami, FL
Description of Spiritual Revelation:

I want to attest to a miracle that happened to me the first time I visited the apparition of the Holy Virgin Mary at the house of Mrs. Rosa Lopez in the city of Hollywood, Florida on November 13, 1994. I had worn around my neck a transparent crystal rosary that I had bought the year before. When I bought it I wanted white, but they didn't have it, so I chose this one, that I liked even more.

When I left the apparition, my rosary had changed and had become as white as pearls. This was a great surprise since I had not requested a miracle because I do not have to see the Virgin Mary in order to believe in Her.

I have just recently remembered that now my rosary looks like the one I originally wanted to buy.

Thank you, Blessed Mother, from your son.

(Signed) *Humberto S. C.*

Date: March 15, 1999
Name: Dolores H. M. (*full name omitted*)
City: Fort Lauderdale, FL
Description of Spiritual Revelation:

The first time I went to Rosa's was October 13, 1994. On October 12, 1994, I was experiencing so much back pain that I thought about going to a chiropractor so I could enjoy my time at Rosa's. I knew that I would have to stand a lot and did not know if I would be able to, in order to say the Rosary. Something inside of me said not to go to the doctor for an adjustment, as I usually did. (In 1983, I lifted a garbage can and twisted my body, injuring some muscles. From 1983 until that October 1994, I was receiving periodic adjustments when my back would go out.)

On October 13, 1994, I went to Rosa's experiencing twinges and discomfort in my lower back, as I had the previous day and other times throughout the years. I went inside the apparition room near the statue of Our Lady. I knelt down and asked Mary if She would ask Her Son, Jesus, to heal my back. I promised to do Her work and that of Her Son, Jesus.

Soon after I said my short prayer, I felt a warm energy moving through my lower back. All the pain did not go away at once, but there was relief. I went outside, sat down on a towel on the grass, and enjoyed the day with slight pain, nothing like the pain I had when I arrived.

Each day I noticed less back pain and my back seemed stronger. At the time, I did not understand why I received a healing, but eventually I did know why Jesus and Mary answered my prayer. Later that year, my mom became very ill and I had to help her, sometimes lifting and supporting her. Had my back not been healed, I could not have been helpful to her.

It is now March 15, 1999, and I have had no pain that would require me to get a back adjustment. It has been more than 4 years since my healing.

Date: May 13, 1999
Name: Eileen G. (*full name omitted*)
City: North Miami Beach, FL
Description of Spiritual Revelation:

I am a 72 year old woman who has had arthritis for the past 12 years. I have been on Lodine, an anti-inflammatory medication. On June 1, 1998, I started to have chest pains and pains in my stomach. I tried different antacids, but nothing helped. I called the doctor for an appointment and got it for the following week.

The doctor examined me and told me I had a stress ulcer from the Lodine, as he had seen other cases like mine from that medication. He gave me another medication to take before meals and it helped a little, but I still had the chest pains and stomach pains.

On July 13, 1998, I went to Rosa's and got there at 11:35 a.m. No sooner did I put my folding chair down, when the loudspeaker came on and announced that Our Holy Mother had arrived early, but that She was not going to give the message yet.

Since I had 5 minutes before we were to start the Rosary, I prayed to Her and told Her about my chest pains and stomach pains and I asked Her to ask Jesus if it was God's Holy Will that maybe I could be cured.

We started the Rosary at 11:45 a.m. We prayed the Joyful Mysteries and were in the middle of the Sorrowful Mysteries, "Jesus Crowned With Thorns", when a woman came out of the house, took the microphone and said, "Excuse me for interrupting the Rosary, but I have a special message from Our Holy Mother for the one out there with the chest pains and ulcer, that you are being cured at this very moment."

I almost fell out of my chair in shock and since that time, my chest pains and stomach pains have disappeared.

(Signed) *Eileen G.*

Date: May 14, 1999
Name: Denise B. (*full name omitted*)
City: North Lauderdale, FL
Description of Spiritual Revelation:

My daughter and I began going to Rosa Lopez's home in October 1997. We heard of the Blessed Mother's visits on the 13th of each month and we wished to become a part of the adoration of the Virgin Mary.

Since attending these apparitions, we have witnessed many miracles and have seen many signs of Her Presence. My daughter has had severe allergies since she was three years old. These allergies required her to receive as many as three shots of medication per week. Since going to Rosa's home and participating in the prayers to Jesus and His Mother, my daughter has not had to go for even one allergy needle. She appears to be cured.

We have witnessed many other miracles during our visits on the 13th of each month. Some of these have been visions of the Virgin Mary, Jesus, and Padre Pio. Others have involved individuals who could not walk prior to the Blessed Mother's appearance, but were able to do so afterward.

When the Blessed Virgin appears each month, the scent of roses in the air is unmistakable. Since we began to pray to Her and say our Rosary daily, we have continually had the scent of roses at our home, also. Through our prayers we have also been blessed personally in many ways over the last six months. We can only attribute these blessings to our renewed faith, which is a direct result of the monthly apparitions.

Date: 1/29/2000
Name: Sharon D. *(full name omitted)*
City: Tamarac, FL
Description of Spiritual Revelation:

For over 3 years, I have had a ruptured disk. I went through several years of therapy, and only surgery was left to be done.

I came to see Rosa in Hollywood, FL and she gave me

a blessing. Now I can bend, walk, and move with no hurting, no problems left. I can now clean my house and walk. I truly received a blessing from Blessed Mary and Rosa.

I am so very grateful.

(Signed) *Sharon D.*

Date: July 4, 2005
Name: Sherry J. G. *(full name omitted)*
City: Sunrise, FL
Description of Spiritual Revelation:

Long before I found out I had breast cancer, my dear work friend Sara told me about this wonder home near her. She explained to me about the apparitions of our Blessed Mother Mary on the 13th of each month.

When I started going to Rosa's home, it helped me to deepen my faith in my Catholic religion. Rosa's home helped me find what was missing in my life, and it was the closeness of my faith. I thank my Lord for helping me to find my way back to Him.

This is the story of my miracle. In March of 2004, there was a large mass in my right breast. My primary doctor sent me for a mammogram, an ultrasound and then to a breast surgeon for a biopsy. By the time the biopsy was done, the tumor had grown very large and it was confirmed to be breast cancer (ductal carcinoma). I went to an oncologist, who recommended six treatments of chemotherapy.

I knew I wanted to see Rosa during this time of difficulty. Rosa blessed me and explained that I needed to come back so I could be blessed several days in a row. Each time Rosa blessed me I could feel the Holy Spirit within her and the love of the Holy Family. She prayed with me and blessed me. She also told be about some things I needed to do to help myself. She gave me Holy Oil to rub on myself and Holy Water to take home to drink.

Whenever I go to Rosa's house I am filled with the spiritual love of God, but the most precious time to go is on the 13th of the month when Our Lady comes to Rosa through Her apparition.

On the 13th of October 2004, I was there in the same room with Rosa during the apparition of Our Blessed Mother. This day was the most blessed day I ever had there. Even though there were many people there that day, I'll never forget that it felt like it belonged to me and Our Blessed Mother Mary. I really cannot explain fully how wonderful it is to be part of something so breathtaking. Everyone needs to experience something like this firsthand. Words can never fully explain how beautiful it is.

Before this day I had already completed my chemotherapy treatments and the surgery had also been done, however, I did not know the outcome of the surgery. I didn't know that my breast surgeon was still worried that they might have to take the whole breast.

When I went back to the surgeon shortly after the 13th for follow-up, he told me that the cancer was all gone. This was wonderful news, but what was even more special to me is what he said next. The doctor said that it was a miracle. Due to the size of the tumor and how fast it had been growing, he hadn't been sure I would live. He said twice that I was a miracle. I knew where this miracle came from. It was through the intervention of our blessed Rosa and the Hands of my Lord Jesus and the Blessed Mother Mary that this miracle was granted to me.

Dear Rosa, I love you so much. Thank you for helping me and blessing me. May God always bless you and keep you safe. You are a very special lady!!

Gratefully,

(Signed) *Sherry G.*

Date: November 8, 2012
Name: Dolores G. (*full name not provided*)
Description of Spiritual Revelation:

In 1995, I went to Rosa's house. I don't remember the month, but I was there on the 13th.

Before going to the house, my doctor told me that I had cancer in my thyroid and a lump in my throat. I was to get surgery on my thyroid and have the lump removed.

The day I went to Rosa's house, I drank Holy Water there. I felt a very cold sensation in my throat (the water was warm). It felt like my throat would burst from being so cold.

Two weeks later, I returned to my doctor for the surgery. It was a 6-hour operation. After the operation, there was no pain at all and I could still talk. The best part is that the doctors could not find any sign of cancer. The lump was removed for biopsy, but no cancer was found in it. I did not have to take any kind of pain medication or thyroid medicine.

Thank you to Jesus and the Virgin Mary and the Holy Spirit! And thank you to Rosa.

I also watched the sun dance and I have several photos from every 13th of the month that I have gone to the apparition site.

(Signed) *Dolores G.*

CHAPTER TEN

The spiritual gifts that were bestowed upon me through visionary Rosa Lopez continue to astound me.

As I continue to repair religious statues, plaques, and paintings, some of which had been broken into fragments, I believe they will be restored through miraculous intervention. Some of them have missing sections that I have to sculpt, craft, or add to.

As I explained earlier, a pivotal moment was when I received the gift of anointing with the Holy Spirit. Unbeknownst to me, this gift would become useful every apparition day, as thousands of people flocked to the site to hear the Virgin Mary's message and seek anointing for physical or spiritual healing.

There were so many people at her house, that Rosa could not accommodate them all, so I and another volunteer were entrusted with assisting her with the blessings.

To this day, I continue to offer this gift. In this role, I am accompanied by Archangel Raphael, who is associated with God's healing power.

It is crucial to clarify that I am not a healer; that I,

myself, cannot heal anyone. My role is simply to present the Holy Spirit to the individuals upon whom I lay hands, and it is entirely their choice whether they accept or reject this gift.

Interestingly, at the moment of anointing, I can discern to some extent whether a person has accepted the Holy Spirit or not. Over the years, I have anointed thousands of people, yet I am unaware of the outcomes of their blessings, as most do not share the results or lack thereof with me.

Allow me to recount some remarkable healing stories I witnessed or was involved in. These incidents occurred at the apparition site and elsewhere, involving encounters with either myself or the visionary, Rosa Lopez, or, as you will soon discover, even without physical contact from anyone at all.

One of the earliest instances of blessings leading to a miraculous outcome took place shortly after the apparitions began in 1994. I first heard about the miracle from Rosa and then had the opportunity to meet the woman involved a few years later, affirming the miracle's authenticity.

The daughter of Cartagena, Colombia's governor/ mayor, was a fashion model who decided to undergo liposuction to regain her pre-pregnancy figure after giving birth to her first child. Tragically, she suffered a stroke during the procedure, and her heart stopped. Though medical professionals managed to revive her heartbeat, she fell into a deep coma. Columbia's top neurologists and surgeons attended to her, but all informed her family that she was brain dead and would never awaken from the coma.

Due to her father's wealth and influence, she was transported to Jackson Memorial Hospital in Miami, and specialists were flown in from California in a desperate attempt to save her life. After a battery of tests, the conclusion remained the same: no brain activity and no hope for recovery.

Devastated, her family was gradually coming to terms with the loss of their beloved daughter when her father's cousin, who had previously visited Rosa, shared the family's story with Rosa and requested her assistance. The cousin asked Rosa if she would accompany her to Jackson Memorial to help this woman, and Rosa agreed.

By this time, the young woman had been in a coma for several weeks. Her body was sustained through intravenous feeding, and she lay curled up in a fetal position.

However, when Rosa entered her hospital room, the young woman miraculously opened her eyes. Rosa proceeded to anoint her and instructed the family to pray for her, assuring them that she would return to anoint her again.

Several days later, Rosa and the cousin returned to the hospital. To their astonishment, when they entered the room, the young woman was sitting up in bed, being fed pudding by her mother. Today, this woman is alive and thriving, although she bears a permanent limp due to weakened muscles on one side.

A few years later, the woman visited the apparition site and shared that she had essentially been trapped within her body. She could hear everything happening around her but couldn't move or speak. She had to relearn how to walk, use utensils for eating, and even communicate verbally. Strikingly, she revealed that the night before Rosa's initial visit, she had dreamt of Rosa entering her room.

This extraordinary healing experience is one of many testaments to the power of faith, prayer, and the intercession of the Holy Spirit working through Rosa Lopez. It exemplifies the profound impact these encounters can have on individuals and their families, providing hope and inspiring a renewed sense of gratitude for life's miracles.

The next miracle I will describe took place at the apparition site while I was present. A heart surgeon affiliated with Miami Hospital began experiencing tremors in his hands. Concerned about it progressing, he sought medical attention and received distressing news from his neurologist: an expanding aneurysm in his brain was pressing on neural pathways, causing the tremors.

Due to the high risks associated with surgery, the doctor was advised to undergo regular monitoring, with the possibility of intervention if the aneurysm grew in size. In the meantime, he was instructed to suspend his surgical practice.

The doctor's parents, who were pilgrims at the apparition site, had already received healing of the father's arthritis, so they encouraged their son to seek assistance from Rosa. But the doctor's pride and scientific background led him to dismiss the idea.

Several weeks passed, and on the next 13th, the doctor went into his office to see a handful of his remaining patients. To his surprise, he was greeted with an unusual situation: each and every one of them had either canceled or rescheduled their appointments. Consequently, he found himself facing a rare occurrence — a day completely unburdened by the usual demands and hectic pace of his bustling practice.

Taking this as a sign, he decided to visit the apparition site, and I had the privilege of sitting next to him that day. When Rosa approached him to anoint his head, she asked him to stand and requested that the volunteers present lay hands on him.

In a spiritual state, he dropped to the floor, remaining in that position for approximately 30 to 40 seconds before opening his eyes.

We helped him to a seat, then Rosa gazed at him intensely, repeatedly asking him if he saw anything. Three times, he responded that he saw nothing. However, the fourth time, with tears streaming down his face, he exclaimed, "What I saw... I should have been dead, for I saw Jesus!" The room erupted in applause, and after prayers and watching Rosa anoint other pilgrims, the doctor left.

The following 13th, the doctor returned to the apparition site again, this time accompanied by his parents. He shared with us that when Rosa and the volunteers laid hands upon his head during his previous visit, he saw Jesus and felt a sharp burning sensation. Days later, the tremors in his hands vanished.

At a follow-up visit with his neurologist, his physician examined a new CAT scan and inquired about his patient's recent surgery. Taken aback, the doctor replied that he had not undergone any surgery. The neurologist then pointed to the scan and revealed the astounding truth: the aneurysm had been repaired, evident by the visible changes on the scan. It was a miraculous healing, attributed not to medical intervention but to the intervention of God, the Divine Physician.

The next two experiences are more testaments to the remarkable healings that occurred through the presence of the Holy Spirit. They are vivid reminders that sometimes the most incredible miracles come at unexpected times, and they reaffirm the awe-inspiring mysteries of Divine intervention.

The following accounts of anointings are ones I performed personally.

In this first instance, a devoted pilgrim arrived at the apparition site very early in the morning, visibly limping with a walking cast on her leg. Concerned, I approached her and inquired about her condition. She explained with some embarrassment that she had torn her Achilles tendon while dancing with her infant granddaughter.

She couldn't stay long that day but hoped to receive a blessing, despite having had medical attention to receive the cast. She also had an upcoming appointment with an orthopedic surgeon.

Aware that Rosa was not yet awake, I offered to pray over her and anoint her in Rosa's stead. She agreed, and during the anointing, a unique experience unfolded. When she directed my attention to the affected part of her body, upon closing my eyes, it seemed as if I could visualize an X-ray of that particular area. I anointed her, and she fell into a spiritual state. Eventually, she regained composure, expressed her gratitude, and departed, unaware of what my mind had witnessed.

It wasn't until the following month that I saw her again. To my amazement, she walked without a cast or any sign of impairment. Delighted, I inquired whether she had undergone surgery. Tears welled in her eyes as she revealed that when she visited the surgeon, he reviewed a fresh set of X-rays and found no tear or damage to her tendon.

To this day, I am humbled beyond belief whenever such healings occur. I continue to anoint and occasionally see similar "x-rays" in my mind.

The second healing I will illustrate occurred one weekend while Christine and I assisted Rosa with visiting pilgrims. The day was a Saturday, and a man we had not seen before arrived with his daughter, a married woman who had been unable to conceive, though fertility testing of her and her husband yielded normal results. Compounding their misery, they were of modest means, which excluded artificial insemination as an option.

Desperate to help, the father brought his daughter to the apparition site to beseech God for a miracle.

Understanding the woman's plight, I offered prayers and anointed her, and the pair left without further contact.

A few months later, during a subsequent 13th, the father sought me out and warmly shook my hand, sharing the wonderful news that his daughter was now pregnant. In humble gratitude, he thanked me, and I expressly reminded him that the miracle was not from me but from the Holy Spirit.

As wonderful as those miracles are, it is essential to acknowledge that not all encounters go as planned. While many instances result in positive outcomes, there are times when unexpected challenges arise.

I vividly recall one particular incident when meeting pilgrims seeking anointing after the message was read. During those encounters, I always wore a Saint Benedict Crucifix as a precaution against evil spirits.

On this occasion, Rosa pulled me aside and discreetly alerted me to a man waiting his turn, informing me that he was tormented by evil. I had seen this man at the apparition site before. I remember him because after receiving multiple blessings, he remained sullen and withdrawn, keeping his head lowered.

When I anointed him, an overwhelming surge of the Holy Spirit coursed through me like never before. However, at the same time, I also felt a force pushing back in defiance. Nauseous and weak, I had to sit down, and Rosa offered me a blessing, silently acknowledging the situation.

Remarkably, this man eventually became a regular visitor to the apparition site, gradually emerging from his shell and engaging with other pilgrims. It is a cautionary reminder that the existence of evil is real, underscoring the importance of spiritual fortitude and vigilance.

Another remarkable miracle that occurred at the apparition site unfolded without direct intervention from the visionary, me, or any of the volunteers. This story was relayed to us by the mother of a young girl who experienced a miraculous recovery from an incurable condition.

Rosa Lopez's house was located at the corner of North 66th Avenue and Arthur Street, a few blocks west of Apollo Middle School. Each morning, the mother would drive her daughter to school and pause at the corner by the house before making a right turn.

One morning, to the mother's surprise, her daughter informed her that the statue atop the fountain at the front of the corner house was speaking to her. The large fountain in front of the house featured a statue of the Virgin Mary on a pedestal. It's important to note that this family was not Catholic and did not actively practice any Christian religion.

Initially, the mother dismissed her daughter's claims as mere fantasy. Additionally, when the daughter persisted in her assertions as the days passed, she grew increasingly annoyed and frustrated.

This continued until one fateful morning when the mother received a distressing call from the school, stating that her daughter had collapsed and had been transported to the hospital.

At the hospital, a neurologist delivered devastating news that no parent ever wants to hear: the young girl had inoperable brain cancer, and her chances of surviving beyond six months were exceedingly slim.

Unable to do more, the doctor advised the mother to take her daughter home the following day and continue their lives as though nothing was wrong. They were instructed to return for weekly checkups, but the decline of her daughter's health was expected to be swift.

Following this grim prognosis, the mother adhered to the doctor's advice, continuing their daily routine of passing by Rosa's house. Each time they drove by, her daughter would affirm that the statue had spoken to her.

One morning, the daughter told her mother that the statue was calling her to visit the fountain and apply some of the water to her head. Not wanting to upset her daughter, the mother pulled off the road and allowed her to approach the statue of the Virgin Mary. There, the girl said she engaged in conversation with the statue and followed its guidance by applying the water over her head.

After the subsequent weekly checkup, the mother visited the house to share her astonishing story with Rosa, whom she did not know. Rosa listened, not completely surprised since she already knew of similar instances of the Virgin's statue interacting with visitors.

The high points of this woman's story, however, were that the girl's most recent MRI had revealed that the cancer in her brain was completely gone, and that neither the woman nor her daughter had had any contact with Rosa or anyone else before that day.

This miraculous healing is yet another testament to the extraordinary nature of faith and the mysterious workings of the Divine. Despite the absence of direct intervention from Rosa or any of the volunteers, the interaction between the young girl and the statue at the fountain brought about an unexplainable disappearance of cancer. This awe-inspiring story again reminds us of the inherent power of belief and the profound potential for miraculous healing if we put our complete trust in God.

CHAPTER ELEVEN

Years after our first visits to the apparition site, I embarked on a path I had never considered before. With Rosa informing me that Archangel Uriel, the bearer of God's wisdom, was at my side, I unexpectedly became a writer and published author. Over time, I also came to recognize the presence of Archangel Gabriel in my writing — the messenger of God who foretold the coming of Jesus.

Permit me now to share the profound influences certain archangels have on our lives. Through research, I have discovered insights into their identities.

One such archangel is Metatron, a spiritual being revealed in the Book of Enoch as holding a position of utmost prominence among all archangels. Metatron, whom Enoch refers to as the Angel, the Prince of the Presence, is entrusted with the guardianship of the sacred tree of life and is responsible for documenting the virtuous acts of every individual. Furthermore, this archangel diligently records celestial happenings within the realm of Heaven.

Metatron is an inexhaustible source of guidance when confronted with uncertain or perplexing decisions. Solace in making informed choices can be found by seeking the counsel of this benevolent angel.

It is also worth noting that Metatron is charged with nurturing children's growth as they transition into adulthood. Additionally, he extends his support to those blessed with spiritual and psychic abilities, rendering assistance and guidance on their respective paths.

In the following paragraphs, I will emphasize the extraordinary qualities of other archangels, including their impacts on various aspects of our lives.

Archangel Gabriel, the strong and divine messenger, radiates power and love. He governs over communication, strength, and new beginnings. He can teach humans to accept and interpret direct messages from the Divine realm. This prominent archangel is recognized by many, as his name, meaning "God is my strength," is found throughout the Bible.

Archangel Raphael, widely acclaimed as the healing angel, carries a name that signifies "he who heals." Among the esteemed archangels recognized by the Church, Raphael champions the cause of the afflicted and those dedicated to their recovery, including pharmacists, nurses, and doctors. His compassionate nature extends to all forms of suffering, encompassing mental, emotional, spiritual, and physical well-being. Raphael stands ready to alleviate distress and offer solace. His responsibilities include bestowing healing and comfort, guiding caregivers, and safeguarding travelers.

Archangel Uriel, my most cherished muse, is often revered as the angel of wisdom. His name is associated with "God is my might" or "Divine fire." As a member of the illuminated seraphim, Uriel occupies a significant position close to the Creator. When grappling with darkness and confusion, Uriel can shed light on God's truth and provide enlightenment. Seeking guidance from Uriel establishes a direct connection with the spiritual realm. Authors and prophets, in particular, hold a special affinity for this awe-inspiring archangel, as his wisdom and insight are invaluable sources of inspiration.

Archangels Metatron, Gabriel, Raphael, and Uriel embody profound forces of guidance, healing, and enlightenment. Embracing their presence can bring about uplifting and transformative changes.

CHAPTER TWELVE

My journey as a writer began in 2006 while I worked as a purchasing manager for a manufacturing company in Fort Lauderdale. Prior to this, I had no intention of becoming an author or writing screenplays. My writing experience had been limited. Business and contract proposals, and an article for a trade paper, were the extent of it.

Though visionary Rosa Lopez had previously identified Archangel Uriel as my muse, this did not incline me to pursue writing. However, after inexplicable promptings from that angel and others, I succumbed. Since then, Uriel and other angelic creatures have enriched my stories and helped me convey their messages to humankind. My main writing muses are now Archangels Uriel and Gabriel, with Raphael by my side during anointings.

I was first inspired to write one auspicious morning when what I considered a brilliant idea for a movie sprung into my mind. Initially, I dismissed it with laughter, labeling it an elaborate story from a dream. However, the idea didn't fade away; it lingered at the back of my thoughts.

Over time, the concept grew in intensity. Soon, I became determined to capture the story doggedly pestering within me. I reached for a notebook and began penning the narrative. As the pages multiplied, I inevitably transitioned to a computer.

I should stop here to explain that years prior, Rosa warned the volunteers that a time would come when churches would be closed — a prophetic revelation of the COVID-19 lockdown — and advised us to display a Bible opened to the Book of Psalms in our homes. Following her advice, Christine and I dedicated a small table to display a Bible, a Crucifix, a statue of the Virgin Mary, and other religious items.

Stemming from this, I developed a routine where I would pause at the Bible before work and on weekends. I would open it randomly and focus on the first passage I saw, considering it my daily inspiration.

One morning, the Bible opened to Luke 21:11, where Jesus foretells events preceding his return, including plagues, earthquakes, and celestial signs: *"There will be great earthquakes, famines and pestilences in various places, and fearful events and great signs from heaven."* **(NIV)**

After reading that passage, I returned the Bible to the Book of Psalms and left it open on the table. Then, I proclaimed **Exodus 15:2-3** from memory, as I continue to do every morning: *"The Lord is my strength and my defense; he has become my salvation. He is my God, and I will praise him, my father's God, and I will exalt him. The Lord is a warrior; the Lord is his name."* **(NIV)**

Dramatically, for three consecutive days, while I continued typing my first creative thoughts into a computer, I opened the Bible to the same passage: Luke 21:11, an occurrence that struck me profoundly. Just like that, it became evident to me that Archangel Uriel was inspiring me on my newfound literary journey.

With this understanding, I veered away from the initial story I was writing and began crafting a very different tale. Comprehending that Archangel Gabriel was also with me, I chose Gabriel as the conduit for delivering God's message to humanity during the weeks leading up to Judgment Day and for portraying the events unfolding in the world as that momentous day approached. Providentially, I titled this book *Gabriel's Chalice*.

Months of rewrites, edits, and publishing preparations followed, and in 2009, the manuscript was finally completed, with the book published in 2011.

Since its publication, *Gabriel's Chalice* has come to be a highly prescient book. Though written before 2009, the story describes plagues, a shortage of hospital resources, and the use of masks, all of which were worldwide experiences during the early days of the COVID-19 virus. The book includes two plagues; one affects the lungs' alveoli, making it difficult to transfer air to the bloodstream, while the other is a side effect of a vaccine intended to combat a different viral invader.

In addition to depicting the plagues we've sadly become familiar with, *Gabriel's Chalice* is proving prophetic in other ways. The story includes lighter-than-air ships, paralleling the current plans of countries like Japan and Spain to incorporate airships into their commercial airline fleets by 2028, coincidentally the same year in which the book's story unfolds. The story also describes massive earthquakes and volcanic eruptions encircling the globe, again similar to recent events.

Gabriel's Chalice marks the first installment of my faith-based sci-fi series, weaving messages of God's Word into a captivating storyline filled with action and intrigue. This book begins the series that takes readers on a journey from the days before the Great Judgment until 1,380 years into the future. Amid gripping narratives, these stories resound with the message that although the Earth will transform, hope will prevail, while simultaneously challenging humanity to embrace change alongside it. Deliberately, the exact nature of the great Day of Judgment remains veiled in the book, as it is known only to the Father.

In this first book, I question whether humanity will learn from past mistakes. I wonder if our pride and greed will wipe out faithfulness to our Creator, forcing us to traverse a path akin to the Israelites' forty-year wandering, a trek that should have lasted no more than ten days.

I continued to assist at the apparition site while writing *Gabriel's Chalice*, and my faith in God and the angels deepened. This reinforcement led me to expand my writing beyond *Gabriel's Chalice* to the third decade after the Great Judgment, a time of global peace.

The second book of my sci-fi series is *Tres Archangelis*, Latin for "three Archangels." In this book, the angels ardently strive to guide humanity back to faith in our Creator during a period when the absence of war fails to guarantee true tranquility. Even though God has issued a commanding decree to the Malignant, commonly known as Satan, demanding that he cease his disruptive interference with humankind, he defiantly ignores God's Divine instruction, much like God's children are consistently prone to do.

In this novel, our compassionate and loving Father foresees the potential threats that could inflict harm or bring about the destruction of His cherished children. In response, he dispatches guardians, celestial beings described as watchers by Enoch, whose sole purpose is protecting humanity from adverse events beyond their control. Notably, since God, in His boundless wisdom, has granted humankind the precious gift of free will, these guardians, while endowed with immense power and wisdom, cannot prevent individuals from making poor choices. Consequently, the guardians can only shield humans from external dangers. They cannot deter the consequences of our own misguided decisions.

In *Tres Archangelis*, God is present among His children, but humans are still unfaithful. They abandon their faith, setting off a chain of events that culminate in the threat of an extinction-level catastrophe on Earth. As a rogue asteroid hurtles toward the planet, persons chosen by God are compelled to seek three keys capable of unlocking the power of the guardians to save humanity.

This narrative illustrates the absolute power of God's will and love and the unwavering certainty of His punishments encompassing humankind, the Malignant, and the entire universe.

According to the Bible, the Great Flood and the coming judgment upon all humanity serve as transformative periods. While God promised never to bring another flood, He did not promise an absence of chastisements. Reflecting on the present state of the world, it becomes apparent that humanity wears self-pride as a badge of honor. Consequently, humans frequently find themselves in a hapless state, seeking to grasp lessons yet unlearned.

In *Xanthe Terra*, the series' third book, God's unconditional, unrelenting, and unwavering patience is again revealed. This novel transports readers to the plains of Mars, a planet I describe in the previous book as one we have tampered with through insatiable greed, pride, avarice, and sin. Through the lens of ongoing archaeological excavations and the discovery of ancient artifacts, I describe a crystal skull that is unearthed and placed upon an ancient pedestal deep within a mountain.

This artifact reveals the tragic tale of God's initial creation, a civilization preceding Adam and Eve, when humans living on Mars, molded in His image, rejected Satan's influence and thrived within their Martian Garden of Eden.

Happily, that civilization prospered. However, hubris eventually took hold, as sadly, it is wont to do, and the culture ended in a catastrophic war between the forces of good and evil.

That clash unleashed terrible and destructive weapons, resulting in mutated monstrous creatures that ravaged the planet's plant and animal life and devoured its people, bringing that entire world to desolation and ruin. By sheer luck, a small group escaped the planet's demise and traveled to Earth, driven by a desperate mission to warn their neighbors not to allow themselves to likewise abandon their faith.

Ultimately, the book shows the group's efforts to be in vain, as centuries later, we accidentally terraform Mars, the planet devastated through the mistakes of God's creatures. In the process of returning that world to a lushness reminiscent of Earth, we inadvertently unleash those ancient monsters again. Our terrible mistake once again demands that humanity relearn the lesson the doomed Martians failed to learn — the fundamental truth that we still fail to comprehend — that we are not superior to, nor on par with, Almighty God.

Sadly, as evidenced by the latest scientific advances in biology, reproduction, artificial intelligence, and other disciplines, this vital lesson continues to elude us, despite repeated reminders.

In August 2018, I took a break from writing when I was diagnosed with prostate cancer. After 43 radiation treatments, I am humbled to say that I am over four years in remission as of this writing, and my muses have not stopped providing me with material.

Therefore, as I initially planned *Xanthe Terra* as the concluding book in my sci-fi series, I have since written one more book as the finale. After the pandemic shutdown, *Samael of Sarah* emerged as a crucial lesson that remained to be taught.

As the final installment, *Samael of Sarah* delves into the rise of the son of Satan, who deceitfully assumes the role of the new messiah. The offspring of a fallen angel and a former human, Samael represents a new breed of Nephilim. The story describes Earth as the battleground for opposing factions, while God, amid the clashes, wearies of His disobedient children and enacts His punishment. This cautionary tale serves as a universal lesson, warning us that God's retribution will surely come if we persist in our destructive ways.

The story depicts the cleansing of Earth, accompanied by three days of darkness. To prepare, God's people are advised to gather candles, food, and water, to cover all windows, and to refrain from gazing upon the outside world. People are instructed to adorn every window and exterior door with a rosary and are warned that the cries for help they may hear from beyond their walls, the pleas from friends and loved ones, and the pounding on their doors, will be the lamentations and temptations of the devil's messengers, seeking to damn souls.

Like the Israelites in bondage who marked their homes and were then spared by the angel of death, humanity will again be allowed to evade death's grasp through a Divine sign bestowed upon God's faithful children.

This story, and others in my series, raise questions about whether we will accept and heed God's warnings. Time will reveal the answer, for God's love is patient, unconditional, and powerful. However, at the same time, His chastisements are absolute, as demonstrated in the Biblical stories of Noah and the Pharaoh, the money changers in the temple, and Ananias and Sapphira. These scriptures warn us to be forewarned, for we err but continually fail to repent.

For anyone who may not know the tragic story of Ananias and Sapphira when they lied to God the Father, I print it here.

Acts 5:1-11: *"But a certain man named Ananias, with Sapphira his wife, sold a possession, and kept back part of the price. His wife, also being aware of it, then brought a certain part and laid it at the apostles' feet. But Peter said, 'Ananias,* *why has Satan filled your heart to lie to the Holy Spirit and to keep back part of the price of the land? While you kept it, didn't it remain your own? After it was sold, wasn't it in your power? How is it that you have conceived this thing in your heart? You haven't lied to men, but to God.' Ananias, hearing these words, fell down and died. Great fear came on all who heard these things. The young men arose and wrapped him up, and they carried him out and buried him. About three hours later, his wife, not knowing what had happened, came in. Peter asked her, 'Tell me whether you sold the land for so much.' She said, 'Yes, for so much.' But Peter asked her, 'How is it that you have agreed together to tempt the Spirit of the Lord? Behold, the feet of those who have buried your husband are at the door, and they will carry you out.' She fell down immediately at his feet and died. The young men came in and found her dead, and they carried her out and buried her by her husband. Great fear came on the whole assembly, and on all who heard these things." (WEBC)*

EPILOGUE

My writing spans several genres, each conveying a profound message while incorporating events that have occurred, could occur, or could realistically transpire. Some of my stories have predicted significant events before they happened, revealing future issues such as presidential impeachments, overt government corruption, and open borders leading to terror attacks in the U.S. I even wrote a narrative in 2018 (published in 2021) that predicted an attempt on the pope's life by someone storming Vatican barricades with a motor vehicle, and this actually happened in May 2023.

The spiritual and physical gifts bestowed upon me through vivid dreams and divine guidance from the Virgin Mary, the Holy Trinity, and Archangels Metatron, Uriel, Gabriel, and Raphael, fill me with a deep sense of humility.

My goal has always been to warn humanity of upcoming events, recognizing that everyone has free will and can choose to do right or wrong.

While challenges come my way, it is through these trials that my connection to God and His angels grows stronger. Some may view my gifts as blessings, while others may see them as a curse. I consider them a great responsibility entrusted to me.

Semper Fidelis, Semper Peratus, Tempus Fugit, Memento Mori.

Matthew 23:31-36: *"Therefore you testify to yourselves that you are children of those who killed the prophets. Fill up, then, the measure of your fathers. You serpents, you offspring of vipers, how will you escape the judgment of Gehenna? Therefore, behold, I send to you prophets, wise men, and scribes. Some of them you will kill and crucify; and some of them you will scourge in your synagogues and persecute from city to city, that on you may come all the righteous blood shed on the earth, from the blood of righteous Abel to the blood of Zachariah son of Barachiah, whom you killed between the sanctuary and the altar. Most certainly I tell you, all these things will come upon this generation."* **(WEBC)**

MIRACULOUS PHOTOGRAPHS TAKEN AT OUR LOVING MOTHER'S APPARITION SITE, HOLLYWOOD, FLORIDA

Our Loving Mother in the clouds over the
Sun with a dazzlingly bright gown.

This is the first photo Our Lady blessed us with at the
apparition site.
Photo credit: unknown. Date: 1995.

Jesus hanging on the Cross in the clouds below the Sun,
similar to the drawing on the left.
Photo credit: Michael (surname unknown).
Date: April 13 (year unknown).

This photo is a gift given to Michael, the fabricator of
the cross that held the large statue of Our Crucified
Lord. After he installed the Cross at the house on
April 10, Rosa told him that Jesus would give him a
gift on the 13th for helping Him in His work.

A luminous Crucifix in the clouds at the apparition site.
Photo credit: Christine Ruffolo. Date: April 13, 1996.

Angels in the clouds above the apparition site.
Photo credit: Christine Ruffolo. Date: April 13, 1996.

A luminous Cross over the Sun.
Photo credit: Frank Ruffolo. Date May 13, 1996.

Large Crucifix in front of Rosa's house.

Tucked under the arm is an image resembling the statue's crucified face facing a different direction. Also, in the upper corner, is a soft green light signifying Our Lord's healing presence.
Photo credit: Rafael (no last name provided). Date: December 1997.

Large profile of Jesus in the clouds.

One Good Friday, Our Loving Mother did not convey a message, but Jesus bestowed upon us a clear image of Himself.
Photo credit: Christine Ruffolo. Date: April 13, 2001.